Reader's Digest
Pathfinders

Dinosaurs

A Reader's Digest Pathfinder

Reader's Digest Children's Books are published by
Reader's Digest Children's Publishing, Inc.
Reader's Digest Road, Pleasantville, NY, 10570-7000, U.S.A.

Visit our web site: www.readersdigestkids.com

Conceived and produced by Weldon Owen Pty Limited
59 Victoria Street, McMahons Point, NSW, 2060, Australia
A member of the Weldon Owen Group of Companies
Sydney • San Francisco

© 1999 Weldon Owen Inc.

READER'S DIGEST CHILDREN'S PUBLISHING, INC.
General Manager: Vivian Antonangeli
Group Publisher: Rosanna Hansen
Editorial Director: Linda Falken
Senior Project Editors: Sherry Gerstein, Beverly Larson
Project Creative Director: Candy Warren
Art Director: Fredric Winkowski
Production Coordinator: Debbie Gagnon
Director of Sales and Marketing: Rosanne McManus
Director of U.S. Sales: Lola Valenciano
Marketing Director: Karen Herman

WELDON OWEN PTY LTD
Chairman: John Owen
Publisher: Sheena Coupe
Associate Publisher: Lynn Humphries
Art Director: Sue Burk
Consultant, Design Concept and Cover Design: John Bull
Design Concept: Clare Forte, Robyn Latimer
Editorial Assistants: Sarah Anderson, Trudie Craig
Production Manager: Caroline Webber
Production Assistant: Kylie Lawson
Vice President International Sales: Stuart Laurence

Author: Paul Willis
Consultant: Michael K. Brett-Surman, Ph.D.
Project Editor: Bronwyn Sweeney
Designer: Karen Clarke
Picture Research: Annette Crueger

Illustrators: Jimmy Chan, Lee Gibbons/Wildlife Art Ltd, Ray Grinaway, Gino Hasler,
David Kirshner, Murray Frederick, David McAlister, James McKinnon, Luis Rey/Wildlife Art Ltd,
Peter Schouten, Peter Scott/Wildlife Art Ltd, Marco Sparaciari, Kevin Stead

Library of Congress Cataloging–in–Publication Data

Willis, Paul M. A.
Dinosaurs / [author, Paul Willis; illustrators, Jimmy Chan ... et al.].
p.   cm. — (Reader's Digest pathfinders)
"A Weldon Owen production" —T.p. verso.
Includes index.
Summary: Introduces dinosaurs, discussing the different categories, what they looked like, what they ate, how we know
about them through the study of fossils, and why they may have become extinct.
ISBN 1-57584-288-2 (hard cover : alk. paper). — ISBN 1-57584-296-3 (lib. bdg. : alk. paper)
1. Dinosaurs—Juvenile literature. [1. Dinosaurs.
2. Fossils. 3. Paleontology.] I. Chan, Jimmy, ill. II. Title. III. Series.
QE862.D5W55462   1999   567.9—dc21   98-53130

Color Reproduction by Colourscan Co Pte Ltd
Printed by Tien Wah Press Pte Ltd
Printed in Singapore

A WELDON OWEN PRODUCTION

Reader's Digest
Pathfinders

Dinosaurs

Reader's
Digest
Children's Books™

Pleasantville, New York • Montréal, Québec

Contents

Introducing Dinosaurs 6

The Dinosaur Parade 26

The Dinosaur Puzzle 44

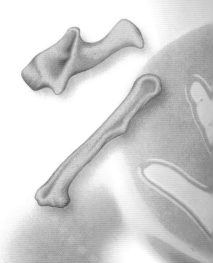

Pick Your Path

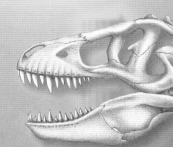

OPEN *DINOSAURS* AND slip back through time on a journey like no other to the prehistoric world of these amazing creatures. Start by learning just what makes a dinosaur a dinosaur, then read straight through to the end and puzzle over why they disappeared from Earth. Or follow your own interests. Want to read about some of the scariest meat-eating dinosaurs? Jump straight to "The Tough Guys" and move through the book from there.

You'll find plenty of other discovery paths to choose from in the special features sections. Read about great dinosaur moments in "Inside Story," or get creative with "Hands On" activities. Delve into words with "Word Builders," or amaze your friends with fascinating facts from "That's Amazing!" You can choose a new path with every reading— READER'S DIGEST PATHFINDERS will take you wherever *you* want to go.

INSIDE STORY
Big Dinosaur Moments

Share the excitement of Paul Sereno and Fernando Novas when they dig up the earliest dinosaur ever found. Join David Gillette as he discovers the remains of the biggest animal ever to walk on Earth. Imagine you're with John Horner when he comes upon 15 nests of fossilized dinosaur eggs and babies—the first evidence that dinosaurs looked after their young. INSIDE STORY lets you feel what it's like to make a discovery and contribute to our knowledge of how the dinosaurs lived and died.

HANDS ON
Create and Make

Find out how many steps you would have to take to keep up with a running *Tyrannosaurus*. Put a chicken's skeleton back together to learn how paleontologists reconstruct dinosaur skeletons. Go hunting for real fossils in the field. Prove to yourself why dinosaurs with long necks had such tiny heads. HANDS ON features experiments, projects, and activities that make the dinosaur world come to life.

Word Builders

What a strange word! What does it mean? Where did it come from? Find out by reading *Word Builders*.

That's Amazing!

Awesome facts, amazing records, fascinating figures— you'll find them all in *That's Amazing!*

Pathfinder

Use the *Pathfinder* section to find your way from one subject to another. It's all up to you!

Ready! Set! Start exploring!

Introducing Dinosaurs

Journey back in time and meet the dinosaurs and the Earth that they ruled for 165 million years. Learn how to tell a dinosaur from a non-dinosaur, and go on a tour of the dinosaurs' world during the Triassic, Jurassic, and Cretaceous periods. Then it's time to get to know dinosaurs a little better—their unique features, their tactics for survival, and their methods of bringing up their babies. Finally, meet the other creatures that lived alongside dinosaurs.

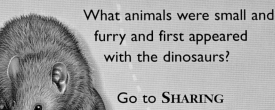

MAGIC DRAGON
People have been digging up dinosaur bones for thousands of years but didn't always know what they were. The Chinese once thought they were dragon bones with magical properties.

What Is a Dinosaur?

WHEN YOU THINK about dinosaurs, you may imagine huge, ferocious creatures—still frightening even though they have been extinct for millions of years. But not all dinosaurs were large. Not all were scary. In fact, an amazing thing about these animals is how different they were from one another. There were some dinosaurs larger than a bus, who romped along on four legs. Others were no bigger than a chicken and cruised about on two legs. Some lived by themselves or in pairs. Others lived in herds of a thousand or more.

Despite their differences, though, dinosaurs had many things in common. They all laid eggs, and they walked with their legs directly under their bodies. Most had scaly skin, like present-day lizards and crocodiles, although some may have had feathers. Dinosaurs can be divided into two groups—those called lizard-hipped and those called bird-hipped, depending on the shape of their hipbones.

Millions of years before our first human ancestors appeared, dinosaurs ruled the Earth. The Age of Dinosaurs lasted 160 million years, during the Mesozoic era. This era is divided into the Triassic, Jurassic, and Cretaceous periods.

DINOSAUR HUNTING GROUNDS
The best places for hunting buried dinosaur bones are the badlands. That's where rivers and streams have eroded layers of rock, making it easier to find the fossils. Dinosaur-rich badlands can be found in the Rockies in the United States and Canada. The badlands in Mongolia are also filled with dinosaur remains.

DEFINITELY NOT A DINOSAUR
The Mesozoic dinosaurs are all dead, so don't let this Komodo dragon fool you. It's the world's largest living lizard. Unlike a dinosaur, it walks with its legs spread out to the side.

EARTH TIME
The history of Earth is divided into eras and periods of time. Different plants and animals were alive at different periods of time. Dinosaurs lived during the Mesozoic era.

Precambrian Time	Cambrian	Ordovician	Silurian	Devonian
			Paleozoic	
4,600 million years ago	550	505	435	408

Word Builders

The word **dinosaur** means "a fearfully great, or terrible, lizard." Sir Richard Owen created the term in 1842 from two ancient Greek words, *deinos* and *sauros*. He needed a name for a new group he had discovered—animals that were often huge, with bodies that looked like lizards.

That's Amazing!

Today we know about more than 800 different types of dinosaurs, and a new type is discovered every seven weeks. Paleontologists think we will eventually find more than 1,000. But there are many dinosaurs that we will never know anything about—they are the dinosaurs that left no fossils behind to tell us about themselves.

Pathfinder

• How were the bird-hipped dinosaurs different from the lizard-hipped dinosaurs? Go to pages 16–17.
• Were dinosaur eggs the biggest eggs ever? Go to page 23.
• How do you start your own fossil collection? Go to page 53.

SPOT THE LOOK-ALIKES

Dinosaurs did not live in the sea. That was the home of marine reptiles. Synapsids, mammal-like reptiles, lived before dinosaurs. Dinosaurs couldn't fly. Pterosaurs, or flying reptiles, did that.

Peloneustes, marine reptile

Dimetrodon, synapsid

Pteranodon, pterosaur

ONE OF MANY

A *Dilophosaurus* lunches on a lizard. This meat-eater of the Jurassic period was almost 20 feet (6 m) long, but it was light and could sprint after prey on its strong back legs. With its fancy head crest, it might have attracted a mate or frightened off a rival.

INSIDE STORY

The Dinosaur Experts

Do you like studying rocks? Have you ever seen a fossil and wondered what it looked like before it became a fossil? Do you love dinosaurs and their prehistoric world? Then becoming a dinosaur expert someday may be just right for you.

You can start now by reading books about dinosaurs and creating your own fossil collection. Fossils are the bits left behind by animals and plants of the past. Most fossils are found in sedimentary rocks.

Dinosaur experts are called paleontologists. They study dinosaur fossils. First they dig the dinosaur fossils up carefully, like these paleontologists. Then they take the fossils to a laboratory where they clean and preserve them. Finally, they study the fossils and discover more about the dinosaurs and the prehistoric past.

Carboniferous	Permian	Triassic	Jurassic	Cretaceous	Tertiary	Quaternary
			Mesozoic		Cenozoic	
50	286	248	208	144	65	2 0

Melanorosaurus

Sellosaurus

Triassic Times

BACK IN THE Triassic period, which started 248 million years ago, the world was one giant supercontinent. It was called Pangaea. The weather was almost always warm, so it was dry like a desert in the middle. But near the coasts, the rain fell and forests of giant ferns sprouted. Most of the animals gathered near the coasts, because that's where they could find plenty of insects and reptiles to eat and plenty of water to drink.

The first dinosaurs appeared about 228 million years ago. They were small meat-eaters that probably evolved from animals no bigger than rabbits. Although they were small, they had one big advantage. Their two back legs let them stand upright and run much faster than the animals they hunted. These speedy killers soon ruled the Triassic world, taking over from the reptiles that had ruled Pangaea before them. Then the first plant-eating dinosaurs started appearing, and they were as big as a pickup truck. By the end of the Triassic period, dinosaurs had spread all over the world. They were bigger and faster and could move more easily than anything else around. And there were no oceans to stop them from spreading across the world.

Pangaea

• Triassic dinosaur site

A VIEW OF THE TRIASSIC WORLD
Pangaea stretched from the North Pole to the South Pole. Triassic dinosaurs could go anywhere they liked in Pangaea without getting their feet wet. Today, the fossils of Triassic dinosaurs have been found on all continents except Antarctica. It's possible to uncover fossils of the dinosaur *Massospondylus* in two such faraway places as southern Africa and Arizona, U.S.A.

A PILE OF OLD BONES
How do scientists find out the age of dinosaur bones? First, scientists identify the type of rock in which the bones were found. Then they compare the bones with other fossils whose age they already know. Last, they find volcanic rock near the bones and measure the rate of decay of the radioactivity in the rock. Scientists used high-tech equipment to determine that these *Coelophysis* bones are about 225 million years old.

Saltopus

Procompsognathus

Word Builders

The word **Pangaea** comes from ancient Greek and it means "all Earth." Pangaea was the only continent in the Triassic period, so all the land in the world was a part of it. The continents we know today—North and South America, Europe, Asia, Africa, Australia, and Antarctica—were joined together in this single, huge landmass.

That's Amazing!

Coelophysis dinosaurs were cannibals. When paleontologists found a big group of *Coelophysis* skeletons at Ghost Ranch in New Mexico, U.S.A., some of them had tiny baby *Coelophysis* skeletons inside their bellies. The babies were the last thing the adults had eaten. But dinosaurs are not the only animals that ate their young. Many other animals still do today.

Pathfinder

• What animals ruled the Triassic seas and skies? Go to pages 24–25.
• What did plant-eating dinosaurs like to eat? What did the meat-eaters eat? Go to pages 28–31.
• Exactly how did dinosaurs end up as fossil bones? Go to pages 46–47.

OTHER INHABITANTS

INSIDE STORY
The Earliest Dinosaur

In 1993, a team of American and Argentinian scientists, led by the famous paleontologists Paul Sereno and Fernando Novas, went looking for the earliest dinosaur. They were searching the harsh badlands of northwest Argentina. As they searched, one of the team was about to throw away a rock when he noticed that it had teeth. He took a second look. The rock contained a fossil skull. Soon he and his colleagues were on the ground, digging up a whole skeleton of an animal that none of them had ever seen before. They knew it was a dinosaur. But how old was it? Was it the first dinosaur?

After months of study, the paleontologists knew it really was the earliest dinosaur ever to be found. They called it *Eoraptor*, meaning "dawn stealer." It was a meat-eating dinosaur, barely as tall as a German shepherd dog, and it lived 228 million years ago.

ON THE GROUND
Animals such as *Kannemeyeria* dominated the first half of the Triassic period. They were synapsids, which were pre-mammals that functioned like reptiles. They survived the dinosaurs' arrival by becoming smaller.

UP IN THE AIR
The earliest creatures to swoop through the world's skies were flying reptiles called pterosaurs. They appeared soon after the first dinosaurs. *Eudimorphodon* was about the size of a large gull. It had wings of skin, like a bat's. It flew over what is now northern Italy.

LIVING SIDE BY SIDE
A plant-eating *Plateosaurus* munches on some ferns in a scene from the late Triassic world. It is about 28 feet (8.5 m) long and has little to fear from two nearby *Coelophysis*. Although they are meat-eaters, the much smaller *Coelophysis* are more interested in catching lizards.

UNDER THE SEA
The oceans were full of marine reptiles like this *Nothosaurus*. Scientists have found fossils of *Nothosaurus* mothers with their babies. The babies were probably born alive, instead of hatching from eggs.

Eoraptor

Herrerasaurus

Jurassic Giants

THE JURASSIC PERIOD started 208 million years ago. This was when the supercontinent Pangaea split in two. The seas rushed in to make two smaller supercontinents, Laurasia and Gondwana. The weather changed, too. It got slightly cooler and rained a lot more. Forests grew thick with tree ferns, cycads, and conifers. This was good food for the plant-eaters, and a good stalking ground for the meat-eaters.

Jurassic conditions were just right for dinosaurs. Many new types flourished. Giant sauropods lifted their long necks to eat from the tallest trees. Armored stegosaurs lumbered about on all fours. Ornithopods no bigger than dogs feasted on undergrowth. Meat-eaters three times as big as an elephant hunted the huge sauropods, while the little meat-eaters scurried after insects and small reptiles.

Dinosaurs were living all over the two continents by the end of the Jurassic period. Those in Laurasia were beginning to look different from those in Gondwana. Most dinosaur groups existed on both continents, but the species were different. Plated *Stegosaurus* roamed North America, while its close relative *Kentrosaurus* lived in Africa.

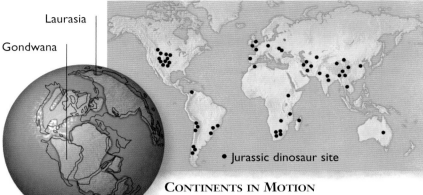

Laurasia

Gondwana

• Jurassic dinosaur site

CONTINENTS IN MOTION
Pangaea broke up into Laurasia and Gondwana, then kept drifting apart. Fossil sites today show Jurassic dinosaurs from the two continents were similar but not the same. Long-necked *Brachiosaurus* found in Colorado, U.S.A., and in Tanzania in Africa look slightly different from each other.

COULD THEY COME BACK?
Dinosaurs are alive again, and some are tracking down tasty humans to eat. That's what happened in the movie *Jurassic Park*. But could it ever happen in real life? The answer is no. The scientists in *Jurassic Park* brought the dinosaurs back to life with a technique called genetic engineering. But to use it, you need dinosaur DNA. We don't have any dino DNA and probably never will. So it seems we won't end up as dino food.

Word Builders

- **Gondwana** means "land of the Gonds." The Gonds were a tribe of people who lived in India (a long time after the Jurassic period, of course).
- **Laurasia** comes from two words, Laurentia—an area on the St. Lawrence River in Canada—and Asia. Laurasia included both Laurentia and Asia.

That's Amazing!

There are Jurassic dinosaur bones buried in Utah, Colorado, and Wyoming, U.S.A., that you can find with a Geiger counter, a machine that clicks when it comes across anything radioactive. It clicks at the Jurassic bones because they contain uranium—but only a small amount, so they're safe.

Pathfinder

- How did meat-eaters kill much larger prey? Go to pages 28–29.
- How big could the Jurassic giants grow? Go to pages 32–33.
- Is it easier for a soft thing like a leaf or a hard thing like a bone to turn into a fossil? Go to pages 46–47.

INSIDE STORY

Plant People

Plants were behind the dinosaur dynasty. Without plants, there would have been no plant-eaters. And no plant-eaters would have meant no meat-eaters. Plants even affected where a dinosaur lived—a big dinosaur couldn't squeeze into a thick forest.

Some plants from the Mesozoic era still grow on Earth today, but most of them haven't been seen for millions of years. The people who know about these vanished plants are paleobotanists such as Bruce Tiffney from the University of California, in Santa Barbara, U.S.A. He is especially interested in the plants that dinosaurs ate and the kinds of environments that plants created for dinosaurs.

He studies fossils like this fossilized hazel leaf to learn about the vanished plants from the world of the dinosaurs.

GROUP ATTACK

A mother *Barosaurus* rears up to protect her baby from an *Allosaurus* attack. The *Barosaurus* could rise up as tall as 50 feet (15 m), and then crash back down to Earth, flattening anything that got in the way of her huge front feet. This scene takes place in a conifer forest of the Jurassic period.

A DINOSAUR DIET

There was plenty of dinosaur food in the Jurassic world. Meat-eaters that didn't eat other dinosaurs gobbled up turtles, crocodiles, lizards, and insects. Plant-eaters liked to nibble on the leaves from ferns and trees. They had many plants to choose from.

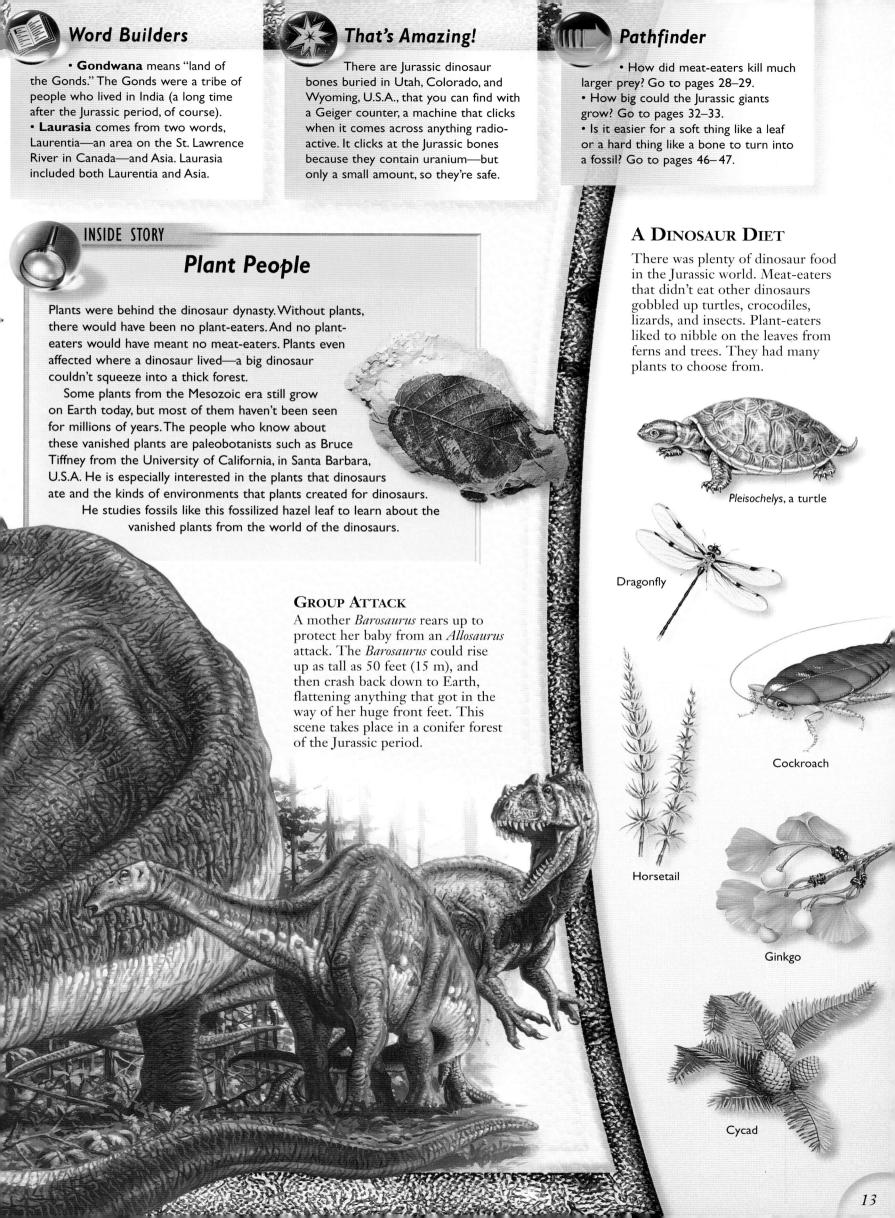

Pleisochelys, a turtle

Dragonfly

Cockroach

Horsetail

Ginkgo

Cycad

Cretaceous Conditions

THE CRETACEOUS PERIOD started 144 million years ago. During that period, the supercontinents of Laurasia and Gondwana kept moving apart, and Gondwana started breaking up into smaller continents. The weather became more seasonal. Summer was warm and wet. In winter, it got chilly. The first flowering plants appeared. By the late Cretaceous period, oaks, magnolias, and hickories covered parts of the Northern Hemisphere. This abundance meant there were more types of dinosaurs than ever before.

Dinosaurs went through many changes during this period. Some, such as the stegosaurs, died out, but armored ankylosaurs took their place. The huge, long-necked sauropods became less common, and new plant-eaters thrived. These included hadrosaurs, with their amazing headgear, and ceratopsians, which looked like rhinoceroses with up to seven horns. And with so much food to feast on, meat-eating theropods like *Tyrannosaurus* appeared.

But after 80 million years, the dinosaurs were all gone. A mass extinction occurred at the end of the Cretaceous period. About 60 percent of all animals died out, including the dinosaurs. It was the end of the Age of Dinosaurs.

• Cretaceous dinosaur site

THE BIG BREAKUP

Laurasia and Gondwana started splitting up into smaller chunks of land. It was harder for dinosaurs to travel between continents. Dinosaurs living in Asiamerica looked more and more different from dinosaurs in Euramerica. There were also more of them than ever before. Finds of Cretaceous dinosaurs are the most common dinosaur fossil sites today.

HANDS ON

Create an Imaginary Dinosaur

Dinosaurs came in some pretty strange shapes. Some of them looked as if they were stuck together from bits of different animals. Have you ever thought about creating your own imaginary dinosaur? What would a *Giraffeodon* look like? How big would an *Elephantosaurus* be?

❶ You will need plain paper and colored pencils to create your imaginary dinosaur. If you need some ideas, look at picture books of birds, reptiles, animals, and dinosaurs.

❷ Draw your imaginary dinosaur on the paper. Take features from real dinosaurs and combine them with characteristics from living animals. Decide what color your dinosaur should be, and then color it in.

❸ Give your dinosaur a name. If you like, write a short history of its life— what it ate, where it lived, and what other dinosaurs lived with it.

Word Builders

- The **Cretaceous** period gets its name from bright white chalk deposits that you can see in the cliffs of southern England. *Creta* is Latin for "chalk," and these chalk cliffs were formed in the Cretaceous period.
- The name **Jurassic** comes from rocks found in the Jura Mountains in southern Germany. These particular rocks date back to the Jurassic period.

That's Amazing!

Cockroaches existed long before dinosaurs, and they're still scuttling around today. That makes them living fossils. A living fossil is an animal or plant that looks the same today as it did when it first appeared in prehistoric times. Some types of crocodiles, lizards, frogs, and turtles are living fossils that first appeared in the Age of Dinosaurs. Some sharks go back even further in time.

Pathfinder

- Do you want to see more hadrosaurs similar to *Corythosaurus*? Go to pages 34–35.
- How did a ceratopsian like *Chasmosaurus* attack? Go to pages 36–37.
- Teams of paleontologists went back to the Gobi Desert in the 1980s. Did they excavate any more dinosaurs? Go to page 50.

PART OF THE SCENE

FIRST FLOWERS
Members of the magnolia family were among the first flowers on Earth. They look almost the same today as when they appeared in the late Cretaceous period. Plant-eating dinosaurs probably ate early flowering plants.

LIZARD LIFE
Lizards and the first snakes were common inhabitants of the Cretaceous period. *Polyglyphanodon* was about the size of a rabbit. It was a food source for small, meat-eating dinosaurs in North America.

INSIDE STORY

Going into the Gobi

Because of its extreme temperatures, the Gobi Desert in Mongolia is one place you probably wouldn't want to live, but it's a great place to visit if you're after dinosaur fossils. Roy Chapman Andrews led four expeditions there between 1922 and 1925 for the American Museum of Natural History. Andrews and his crew drove a caravan of camels and cars, packed full of supplies. They fought off bandits, battled sandstorms, and found hundreds of dinosaur fossils. They dug up a nest of dinosaur eggs, the first ever found. They also discovered dinosaurs such as *Oviraptor*, *Protoceratops*, *Saurornithoides*, and *Velociraptor*. The fossils were taken to the Museum for study and are on display there today.

ANCIENT MAMMALS
The early mammals were common by now. Mammals never got any bigger than cats during the Cretaceous period. One was *Crusafontia*, which made a tasty snack for smaller, meat-eating dinosaurs.

HERD APPROACHING
A herd of crested *Corythosaurus* and horned *Chasmosaurus* thunders across a plain in North America. These plant-eating dinosaurs are making their annual migration in search of new food. A herd could have had more than 10,000 dinosaurs. Meat-eaters such as *Tyrannosaurus* lurked behind, ready to attack any weak or sick animals.

Pachycephalosaurus

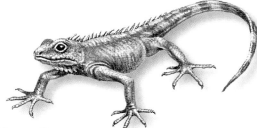

Lizard-hipped **Apatosaurus**   *Bird-hipped* **Wuerhosaurus**

The Two Hip Groups

A DINOSAUR COULD belong to one of two different groups, depending on what type of hips it had. The saurischian group had hips that looked like a lizard's, so they are called the lizard-hipped dinosaurs. Ornithischians had birdlike hips. They're the bird-hipped dinosaurs.

All the meat-eaters belonged to the lizard-hipped group. Some plant-eaters also belonged, such as the long-necked sauropods and their smaller ancestors, the prosauropods. All the other plant-eaters were bird-hipped. They had a pubis bone in their hips that pointed backward. That left more space for a big stomach and intestine, which they needed to digest the plants they ate.

Although saurischians and ornithischians had different hips, their hipbones connected to their leg bones in exactly the same way. A right-angled joint meant that they could walk with their legs straight under their bodies, instead of sprawling—the first animals ever able to do this. They used up less energy than the sprawling animals so they could grow bigger, walk farther, and run much faster than anything else around. The straight-walking stance of the dinosaurs was the secret of their success.

LEGS OUT
Lizards sprawl when they walk. They have to twist their whole body and lift each leg one at a time. This takes a lot of energy and can be used only for short bursts of speed.

UNDER OR OUT
Young crocodiles have an upright stance for walking. But once they have grown, crocodiles sprawl their legs out like other reptiles.

HANDS ON

A Skeleton Puzzle

When paleontologists have a pile of dinosaur bones and want to put them together, it's like solving a jigsaw puzzle. If they put the bones together correctly, they get a dinosaur skeleton. You can put together a skeleton, too, next time you have cooked chicken.

❶ Keep all the chicken bones. Ask your parents to boil them so they are clean. Then place the bones on a flat surface.

❷ Look at the bones. Think about how they go together to form a skeleton. The legs and wings are long, straight bones. Curved ribs form a cage in the chest. The hipbones are flat, a platform for the legs. The back has many small, squarish bones called vertebrae. Can you solve the puzzle and put the chicken skeleton back together again?

DIFFERENT HIP BITS

A dinosaur's hips had three bones. The pubis and ilium supported leg muscles, and the ischium supported tail muscles. The two types of dinosaur hips are easy to tell apart. In the lizard-hipped group, the pubis pointed forward, and in the bird-hipped, it pointed backward.

ilium

ischium

pubis

LIZARD-HIPPED
Oviraptor was a meat-eating dinosaur and a typical saurischian. Its pubis pointed forward, sticking out by itself to make a triangle with the other two pelvic bones, the ilium and ischium.

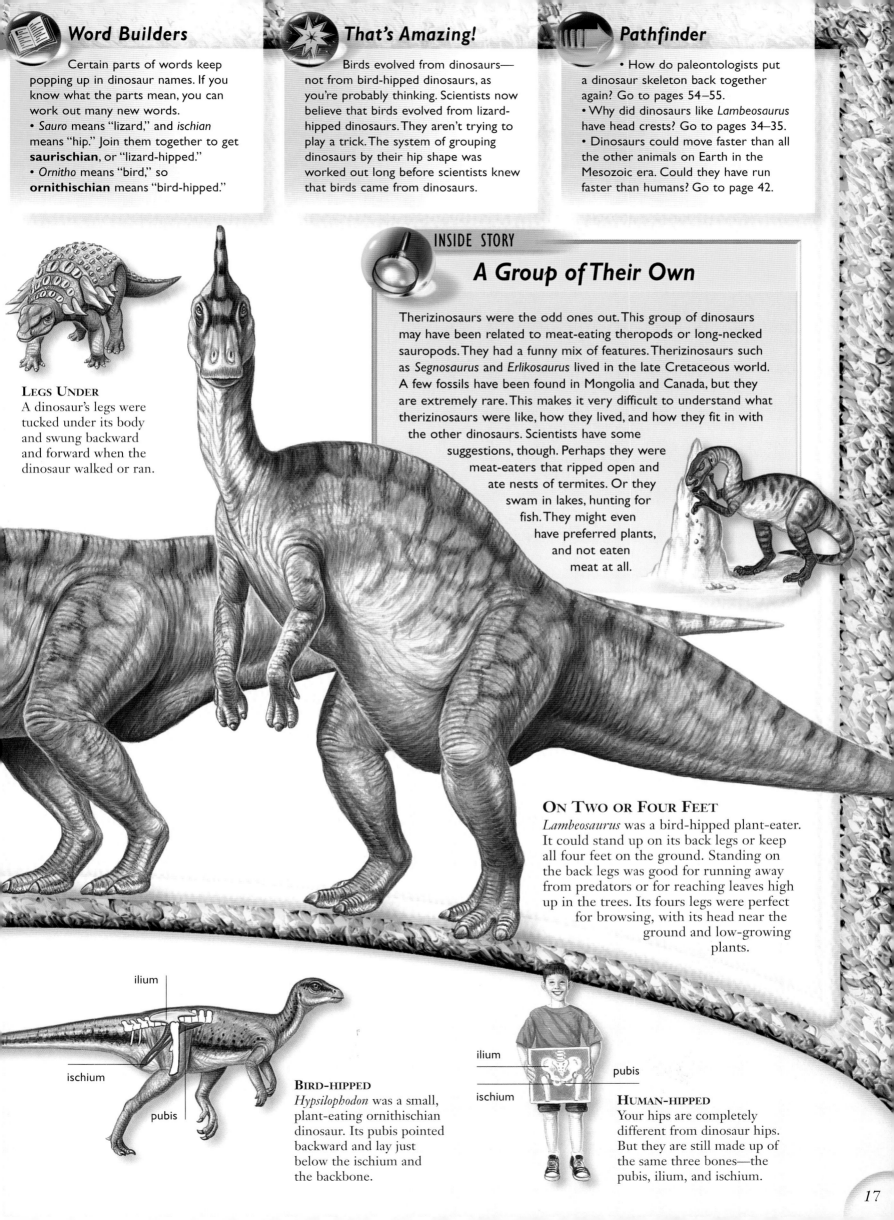

Word Builders

Certain parts of words keep popping up in dinosaur names. If you know what the parts mean, you can work out many new words.
• *Sauro* means "lizard," and *ischian* means "hip." Join them together to get **saurischian**, or "lizard-hipped."
• *Ornitho* means "bird," so **ornithischian** means "bird-hipped."

That's Amazing!

Birds evolved from dinosaurs—not from bird-hipped dinosaurs, as you're probably thinking. Scientists now believe that birds evolved from lizard-hipped dinosaurs. They aren't trying to play a trick. The system of grouping dinosaurs by their hip shape was worked out long before scientists knew that birds came from dinosaurs.

Pathfinder

• How do paleontologists put a dinosaur skeleton back together again? Go to pages 54–55.
• Why did dinosaurs like *Lambeosaurus* have head crests? Go to pages 34–35.
• Dinosaurs could move faster than all the other animals on Earth in the Mesozoic era. Could they have run faster than humans? Go to page 42.

LEGS UNDER
A dinosaur's legs were tucked under its body and swung backward and forward when the dinosaur walked or ran.

INSIDE STORY

A Group of Their Own

Therizinosaurs were the odd ones out. This group of dinosaurs may have been related to meat-eating theropods or long-necked sauropods. They had a funny mix of features. Therizinosaurs such as *Segnosaurus* and *Erlikosaurus* lived in the late Cretaceous world. A few fossils have been found in Mongolia and Canada, but they are extremely rare. This makes it very difficult to understand what therizinosaurs were like, how they lived, and how they fit in with the other dinosaurs. Scientists have some suggestions, though. Perhaps they were meat-eaters that ripped open and ate nests of termites. Or they swam in lakes, hunting for fish. They might even have preferred plants, and not eaten meat at all.

ON TWO OR FOUR FEET
Lambeosaurus was a bird-hipped plant-eater. It could stand up on its back legs or keep all four feet on the ground. Standing on the back legs was good for running away from predators or for reaching leaves high up in the trees. Its fours legs were perfect for browsing, with its head near the ground and low-growing plants.

ilium
ischium
pubis

BIRD-HIPPED
Hypsilophodon was a small, plant-eating ornithischian dinosaur. Its pubis pointed backward and lay just below the ischium and the backbone.

ilium
pubis
ischium

HUMAN-HIPPED
Your hips are completely different from dinosaur hips. But they are still made up of the same three bones—the pubis, ilium, and ischium.

What's Cool? What's Hot?

IF ANIMALS GET too hot or too cold, their bodies can't work properly. Animals feel best when their body temperature is just right. They regulate their body temperature in two different ways. Cold-blooded animals, such as lizards and snakes, get their body heat from outside. They sunbathe until they warm up, then they move into the shade. Warm-blooded animals, such as humans and other mammals, generate heat inside their bodies. They convert energy from the food they eat into heat to keep warm.

It seems that the dinosaurs did it both ways. Some dinosaurs were probably "cold-blooded." They lived in warmer climates, where it was easy for them to keep warm. Their huge bulk held heat in to get them through cold days. Some had sails, plates, and frills—good for soaking up the Sun, then cooling off again. The long-necked dinosaurs had lots of skin to let off steam fast so they didn't overheat.

Small dinosaurs were more likely "warm-blooded." Warm-blooded dinosaurs were able to live in cold or hot places, so long as they could get enough to eat. That's the way they fueled their internal fires, keeping warm and busy by eating plenty of food.

DINOSAURS IN THE DARK
Leaellynasaura lived in southern Australia during the Cretaceous period. The days would have been dark and freezing cold during the winter months. *Leaellynasaura* was too little to migrate. It must have been warm-blooded to survive in a place where the Sun didn't shine.

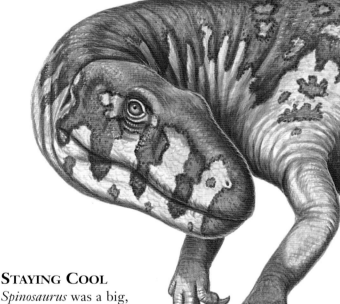

STAYING COOL
Spinosaurus was a big, meat-eating dinosaur. Because it lived in a hot place, it had no trouble getting warm. But keeping cool would have been a problem without the sail on its back. It may have acted like a built-in cooling plant. When things got too hot, the dinosaur may have stood in the shade and pumped warm blood into the sail, where the blood cooled down before going back into the body.

INSIDE STORY
Not So Slow After All

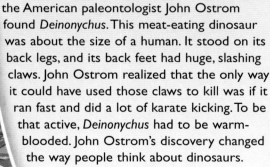

All dinosaurs were big, dumb, cold-blooded creatures that thudded along slowly. That's what everyone used to think, until the American paleontologist John Ostrom found *Deinonychus*. This meat-eating dinosaur was about the size of a human. It stood on its back legs, and its back feet had huge, slashing claws. John Ostrom realized that the only way it could have used those claws to kill was if it ran fast and did a lot of karate kicking. To be that active, *Deinonychus* had to be warm-blooded. John Ostrom's discovery changed the way people think about dinosaurs.

BONES UNDER THE MICROSCOPE
Warm-blooded and cold-blooded animals have different growth patterns. You can see the differences in their bones if you use a powerful microscope. Paleontologists look for these differences in dinosaur bones, too.

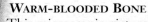

WARM-BLOODED BONE
This microscopic picture of a dinosaur bone looks similar to pictures of mammal bones. So maybe this dinosaur was warm-blooded like modern mammals.

Word Builders

• An **ectotherm** is an animal that gets its heat from outside its body. This name comes from *ektos,* meaning "outside." Ectotherm is one technical name for a cold-blooded animal.
• An **endotherm** is an animal that generates heat inside its body. *Endon* means "within." Endotherm is a term for warm-blooded animals.

That's Amazing!

Feathers and fur are so soft, they hardly ever get preserved as fossils. But scientists recently dug up some dinosaur fossils in China and found small, meat-eating dinosaurs that had feathers. Maybe they were warm-blooded, like birds, and the feathers helped keep them cozy.

Pathfinder

• Do you want to see a *Deinonychus* ready to attack? Go to pages 28–29.
• Just how fast could warm-blooded dinosaurs travel? Go to pages 42–43.
• What would have happened to the dinosaurs if the weather had gotten too hot or too cold? Go to page 59.

Thin skin allowed heat to spread quickly.

Long bones held up the huge back sail.

Blood vessels filled the sail, letting blood cool down.

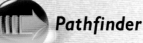

HANDS ON
Warming Up on a Cold Day

You can get some idea of how long it would have taken a cold-blooded dinosaur to warm up, compared to a warm-blooded dinosaur. All you need is a watch to time yourself. Then bundle up and go outdoors on the next cold but sunny day.

❶ First, pretend you're a slow, cold-blooded dinosaur that can't find a sunny spot. Stand still in the shade. How long does it take to feel warm? Or do you feel colder the longer you stand there?

❷ Now stand still in a sunny spot. Do you get warm? How long does it take?

❸ Run around outside, like an active, warm-blooded dinosaur would. Stop when you're nice and warm. Check how long it takes. How much energy do you use? That's another thing you can check: Are you very hungry, a little hungry, or not hungry at all?

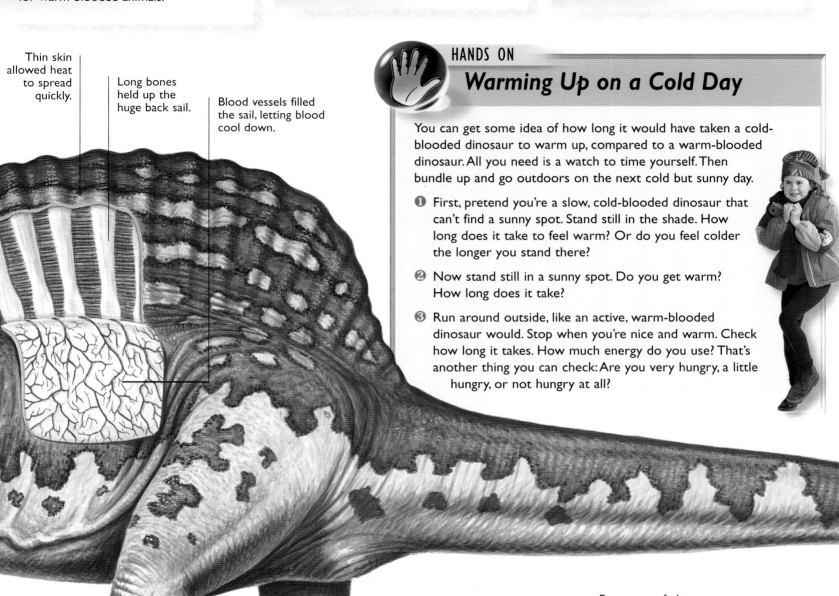

Bony core of plate

Blood vessels

Thin skin covering

HOT PLATES
Stegosaurus had back plates packed full of blood vessels. It may have turned its plates to face the Sun to warm its blood before it was pumped to the rest of the body. To cool the blood, *Stegosaurus* may have turned the thin edge of its plates to the Sun.

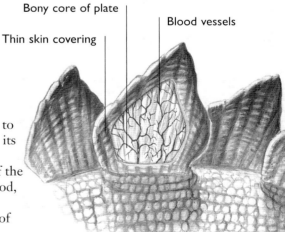

QUICK-GROWING BONE
Birds and mammals have bones like this dinosaur bone. Such bones form those parts of the skeleton that grow quickly when the animal is young.

COLD-BLOODED BONE
The rings in this dinosaur bone are like those in reptile bones. Rings form because cold-blooded animals grow more slowly in winter, as their temperature drops.

Survival

IT WAS A daily fight for survival in the dinosaur world. Plant-eaters and meat-eaters had to find enough to eat while making sure they didn't get eaten themselves. They used a range of defensive strategies and plans of attack.

Plant-eaters concentrated on defense. Many had horns, armor, spikes, or tail clubs to protect themselves from hungry meat-eaters. Small and speedy *Hypsilophodon* could dodge out of harm's way. Sauropods like *Barosaurus* used their sheer size and their whiplike tails to keep predators at a distance. They and many other plant-eaters stuck together and moved about in herds. A gang of horned *Triceratops* could easily intimidate a lone predator.

Meat-eaters went on the attack. They needed an array of weapons and tactics to capture and kill their prey. First, they had to get up close, perhaps by using camouflage. Large theropods like *Tyrannosaurus* probably hunted alone or in small groups of two or three, hiding until the time was right for an ambush. Smaller *Velociraptors* worked in teams, chasing or trapping an animal. After capture came the kill. Most meat-eaters used claws or teeth to deliver the final, fatal wounds. Their tools for defense were the same as their tools for attack: speed, surprise, and sharp teeth.

READY FOR IMPACT
Pachycephalosaurs had thick, bony heads and skeletons that could go rigid. This may have helped in head-butting attacks against predators or competition among males during fights for dominance.

INSIDE STORY

Caught in the Act

It's rare to find evidence of a dinosaur fight, but that's exactly what paleontologists discovered in a Mongolian desert. Millions of years ago, a hungry *Velociraptor* attacked a *Protoceratops*. While fighting, the dinosaurs tumbled down a sand dune. The dune collapsed on top of them, killing them both and preserving them just as they were at the moment of death. When the fossil of the dinosaurs was dug up, the teeth and beak of the *Protoceratops* were still clenched around the arm of the *Velociraptor*. The deadly killing claw on the left foot of the *Velociraptor* was buried deep in the stomach of the *Protoceratops*. The two dinosaurs had remained locked in battle for 80 million years.

CAMOUFLAGE COLORS

We don't know what colors dinosaurs came in. But we know what environments they lived in. We also know that the right colors help an animal to hide in its surroundings, camouflaged from both predators and unwary prey. We can look at animals living in similar environments today for clues about dinosaur colors.

STRIPES
Coelophysis was a swift predator like a tiger. Perhaps *Coelophysis* also had stripes like a tiger. Stripes help camouflage an animal's shape–so its prey may not see it coming before it strikes.

Word Builders

- If something is ankylosed, it is fused together. **Ankylosaurus** means "fused lizard." It's the name of the dinosaur with an armor of bone that was fused together to protect its body.
- **Pachycephalosaurus** means "thick-headed lizard." It gets its name from the Greek words *pachys*, meaning "thick," and *kephalos*, or "head." This dinosaur had a thick, bony head.

That's Amazing!

How long could a dinosaur live? We don't know for sure, but it helps to look at animals alive now. If dinosaurs lived and grew at the same rate as crocodiles, the biggest dinosaurs would have lived over 300 years. If they were like elephants, then the biggest probably lived to 100. Small dinosaurs would have lived only about five years.

Pathfinder

- How did *Velociraptor* hunt in a pack? Go to page 29.
- Do you want to see a whole range of dinosaurs with horns, spikes, clubs, and armor? Go to pages 36–37.
- How do scientists know what color dinosaurs were? Go to page 56.

FOSSIL FIGHT
A *Dromaeosaurus* attacks a *Lambeosaurus*. These two skeletons have been reconstructed in this realistic pose to show what would have been a fight to the death.

WHIPPED
Diplodocus had a tail that was almost as long as a tennis court and that worked like a whip. *Diplodocus* used its tail to lash out at attackers with stinging blows.

ON THE ATTACK
The *Ankylosaurus* stands its ground and takes a swipe at an attacking *Tyrannosaurus* with its tail. One direct hit to the ankles by the massive bony club on the end could cripple the *Tyrannosaurus*. Sharp studs and slabs of bone protect the back of *Ankylosaurus*, but one bite to its soft underbelly from the powerful meat-eating jaws of *Tyrannosaurus* would finish it off.

SPIKED
Tuojiangosaurus had a serious set of tail spikes. With one swing of its tail, this plant-eater could puncture a predator's belly.

SPOTS
Dryosaurus was a small plant-eater that lived in forests, as many deer do today. Deer have light spots on a darker background, similar to the dappled light in forests. *Dryosaurus* perhaps had spots, too.

PLAINS COLORS
Edmontosaurus lived in herds and migrated across continents, the same way antelopes do today. Antelopelike colors may have helped *Edmontosaurus* blend in on the open plains.

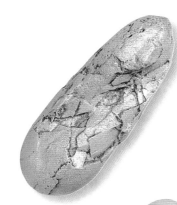
The Next Generation

DINOSAURS LAID EGGS, like birds and most reptiles. The first dinosaur eggs were found in France in 1859. Then nests full of eggs were uncovered in Mongolia in the 1920s. But what about the parents? Paleontologists decided that dinosaurs didn't stay around to look after their young. They just built the nests, laid the eggs, then left—the same as most turtles, lizards, and snakes today.

That thinking changed in 1978, when John Horner dug up a duck-billed dinosaur nursery near Choteau, in Montana, U.S.A. The nests full of *Maiasaura* eggs were built close together, but there was enough space for the parents to move about, guard the nest, and not squash anything. The babies had worn-down teeth, and the eggshells they had hatched from were broken up. This meant they must have stayed in their nests, being fed and cared for by their parents, until they were ready to leave.

Paleontologists have found more fossil eggs, from giant sauropods and small meat-eaters like *Oviraptor* and *Troodon*. Each dinosaur had its own type of eggs and nests and way of doing things. But most of them were more like birds than reptiles when it came to caring for their young.

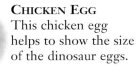

OVIRAPTOR EGG
This long, thin egg belongs to an *Oviraptor*. Shallow grooves run along its length. Millions of years ago, it got squashed somehow and fossilized that way.

CHICKEN EGG
This chicken egg helps to show the size of the dinosaur eggs.

FUTURE HERBIVORE
This round, squat egg has a pimpled surface. It probably belonged to a plant-eating dinosaur.

FEEDING TIME
A mother *Oviraptor* returns to her nest of hungry babies. She has a freshly killed baby *Velociraptor* for their dinner. *Oviraptor* means "egg thief," because the first *Oviraptor* fossil was found near a nest of eggs. Scientists initially thought that the nest belonged to another dinosaur and that the *Oviraptor* had been stealing the eggs to eat. But now we know that the nest actually belonged to the *Oviraptor*. She was looking after her unhatched babies.

INSIDE STORY

The Egg Man

Baby dinosaurs are extremely rare. So when John Horner, field paleontologist at the Museum of the Rockies, came across a baby dinosaur fossil in a rock shop in Montana, U.S.A., he went looking for where it had come from. He and his team ended up in the badlands of Montana, uncovering a nest of crushed eggshell and 15 duck-billed babies, each about 3 feet (1 m) long. The team eventually found a whole breeding ground that contained 15 nests of *Maiasaura* eggs and babies— and the first evidence that dinosaurs looked after their young.

The discoveries didn't stop there. At Egg Mountain, Dr. Horner found nests and eggs of *Orodromeus*. These babies needed less care than *Maiasaura* babies. He and his team have found more than 500 dinosaur nests, plus a herd of 10,000 dinosaurs that died in a volcanic eruption. And he's still out there looking.

CRACKING THE EGG CODE

THE LINEUP
Dinosaurs had different ways of laying their eggs. Some small meat-eaters laid pairs of eggs side by side to form two lines. The eggs were usually half-buried in the nest.

IN AN ARC
The sauropods laid their eggs in an arc across the ground. They laid the first egg, then moved their back legs around a little (their front legs always stayed in the same spot) to lay the next egg, and so on. They don't seem to have built any nests.

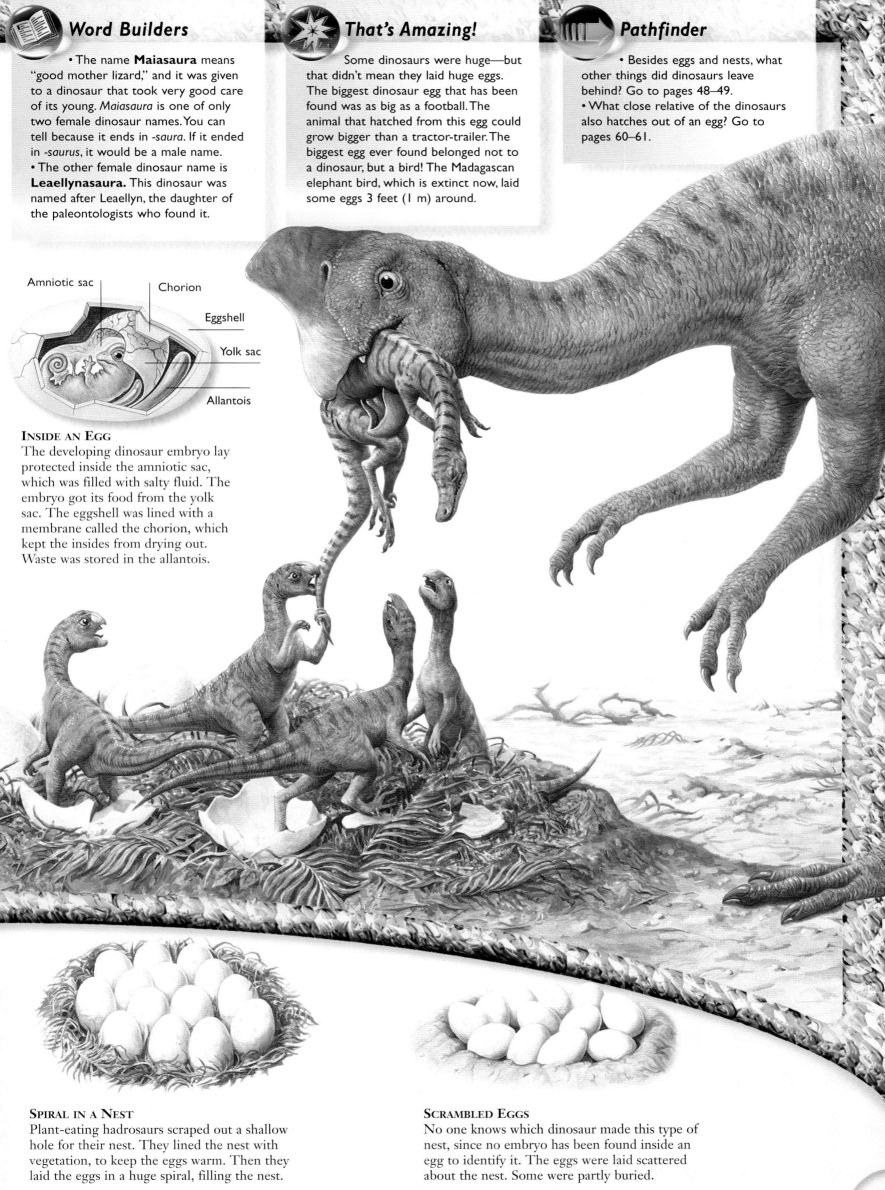

Word Builders

• The name **Maiasaura** means "good mother lizard," and it was given to a dinosaur that took very good care of its young. *Maiasaura* is one of only two female dinosaur names. You can tell because it ends in *-saura*. If it ended in *-saurus*, it would be a male name.
• The other female dinosaur name is **Leaellynasaura**. This dinosaur was named after Leaellyn, the daughter of the paleontologists who found it.

That's Amazing!

Some dinosaurs were huge—but that didn't mean they laid huge eggs. The biggest dinosaur egg that has been found was as big as a football. The animal that hatched from this egg could grow bigger than a tractor-trailer. The biggest egg ever found belonged not to a dinosaur, but a bird! The Madagascan elephant bird, which is extinct now, laid some eggs 3 feet (1 m) around.

Pathfinder

• Besides eggs and nests, what other things did dinosaurs leave behind? Go to pages 48–49.
• What close relative of the dinosaurs also hatches out of an egg? Go to pages 60–61.

Amniotic sac
Chorion
Eggshell
Yolk sac
Allantois

INSIDE AN EGG
The developing dinosaur embryo lay protected inside the amniotic sac, which was filled with salty fluid. The embryo got its food from the yolk sac. The eggshell was lined with a membrane called the chorion, which kept the insides from drying out. Waste was stored in the allantois.

SPIRAL IN A NEST
Plant-eating hadrosaurs scraped out a shallow hole for their nest. They lined the nest with vegetation, to keep the eggs warm. Then they laid the eggs in a huge spiral, filling the nest.

SCRAMBLED EGGS
No one knows which dinosaur made this type of nest, since no embryo has been found inside an egg to identify it. The eggs were laid scattered about the nest. Some were partly buried.

Sharing Dinosaur Space

DINOSAURS DOMINATED THE land during the Mesozoic era, leaving the air and the oceans to other creatures. Flying reptiles soared through the skies. Marine reptiles patrolled the seas. Some of these reptiles might have looked a bit like dinosaurs, but they were only very distant cousins.

Before birds there were the pterosaurs, the flying reptiles of the Mesozoic era. They could be as small as a seagull or as big as a biplane. Their very fine bones kept their bodies light enough to fly. They glided or maybe even flapped about on wings of skin, their large eyes on the lookout for fish and small animals to eat.

Under the oceans it was just as busy. Different types of marine reptiles competed to feed on fish, small sea creatures, and each other. The dolphinlike ichthyosaurs were fast predators, torpedoing through the water. The plesiosaurs swam more slowly, using four flippers to push their barrel-like bodies along. Their small heads flicked from side to side on their long necks as they searched for fish. The pliosaurs had much larger heads and short necks. They were the killer whales of the Mesozoic seas. Turtles, sea crocodiles, and sea dragons, or mosasaurs, were there too. Their relatives are still around today.

ICHTHYOSAURUS
With its dolphinlike shape, this fishlike reptile could swim at high speeds.

LIOPLEURODON
This typical pliosaur had a long head and short neck.

BERNISSARTIA
Crocodiles like this were the cousins of the dinosaurs, and were common at this time.

INSIDE STORY
65-Million-Year-Old People?

A man rides a *Barosaurus* to work. Kids slide down a *Diplodocus*'s tail. People live side by side with dinosaurs. You've probably seen it in *The Flintstones*, or read about it in *Dinotopia*. But it never happened. The last dinosaur died 65 million years ago. The first humans didn't appear on Earth until some time during the last million years.

Our distant relatives were there during the Mesozoic era, though. The early mammals were no bigger than cats and they looked a little like rats, but they were the dinosaurs' next-door neighbors. And there are some descendants of the dinosaurs living with us humans today—the birds. But there's no confusing a turkey with a *Tyrannosaurus*.

Elasmosaurus, *a plesiosaur*   Kronosaurus, *a pliosaur*

Word Builders

• *Plesio* means "similar" or "close to," so **plesiosaur** means "similar or close to a lizard." This group got its name because scientists used to think plesiosaurs were closely related to crocodiles. Now we know they're not.
• *Ptero* means "wing." **Pterosaur,** meaning "winged lizard," is the name of the group of reptiles that could fly.

That's Amazing!

Quetzalcoatlus was a pterosaur, the biggest animal ever to fly through the air. It had a wingspan as wide as 45 feet (14 m). That's wider than the wingspan of many small planes! *Quetzalcoatlus* probably didn't flap its wings of skin to get about. Instead, it would have stretched them wide to soar on air currents, like a glider.

Pathfinder

• Why is a plesiosaur not a dinosaur? Go to pages 8–9.
• Birds didn't evolve from pterosaurs. How did they evolve? Go to pages 60–61.

EVOLVING AT THE SAME TIME

The Mesozoic world had other creatures living alongside the ruling reptiles.

SNAKES AND LIZARDS

Pachyrhachis was one of the earliest known snakes. It lived in what is now Israel during the Cretaceous period. Snakes as well as lizards developed during the Mesozoic era.

BUILT FOR FLIGHT

This fossil of *Rhamphorhynchus* shows how lightly built the bodies of pterosaurs were. You can also see the wings of skin, which stretched from its body to the very tip of its incredibly long fourth fingers.

MOTHS AND BEES

While many groups of insects had already evolved, tiny moths and small social bees were two groups that first appeared with the dinosaurs.

DANGER ON ALL SIDES

A *Scaphognathus* dive-bombs through late Jurassic skies over what is now Europe. It is headed for the same school of *Pholidophorus* fish that a 13-foot (4-m) plesiosaur, *Cryptoclidus*, is after. The end of *Scaphognathus*'s long tail was shaped like a leaf. It probably acted like a rudder, helping *Scaphognathus* steer through the air. You can still find fossils of these creatures in rocks in southern England.

Archelon, *a turtle*

Platecarpus, *a mosasaur*

MAMMALS

Warm-blooded mammals got their start in the Age of Dinosaurs. But they stayed small for most of that time, like the *Alphadon* above.

The Dinosaur Parade

From a safe distance, you can see the many different dinosaurs that crashed or scurried through the Age of Dinosaurs. First view meat-eaters, the fierce killers who dominated the dinosaur world in their search for prey. Then look at all the different plant-eaters—some with long necks and others with strange headgear or spikes, clubs, and plates of bony armor. Stop to take in the biggest and smallest, and finish up with the fiercest and fastest among all the dinosaurs.

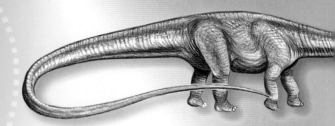

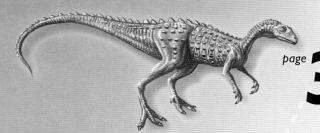

page **36** Would a dinosaur such as *Scutellosaurus* usually stand and fight, or make a run for it?

Where was the one soft spot in *Sauropelta*'s bony armor?

Go to THE ARMORED DIVISION.

page **38** This shows a boy compared to the smallest meat-eater. How would the boy compare to the biggest meat-eater?

Go to BIG AND SMALL.

page **40** What dinosaur had a huge mouth with more than 50 stabbing teeth?

One dinosaur's killer claws had a special feature. What was it?

Go to THE TOUGH GUYS.

page **42** Who would win the race between the fastest human in the world and the fastest dinosaur?

How do we know that this dinosaur could run at 40 miles (64 km) per hour?

Go to THE FAST MOVERS.

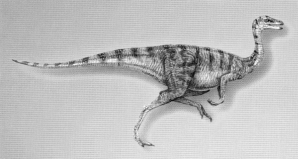

The Meat-Eaters

MEAT-EATING DINOSAURS WERE lean, mean, killing machines. Their bodies were designed to capture, kill, and tear apart prey. They gave chase on two strong back legs, and some grabbed their prey with their hands. If there was a struggle, the large, curved claws on their hands and feet could pierce skin to get a grip on slippery flesh. For the final kill, most carnivorous dinosaurs chomped down with their mouthful of murderously sharp teeth, then used those same teeth to tear their food into bite-sized pieces.

Meat-eating theropods dominated the dinosaur world in the quest for food. Some ate other dinosaurs, usually plant-eaters. Some liked meals of small mammals, lizards, or insects. The dinosaur's diet depended a lot on its size.

Theropods such as *Tyrannosaurus* and *Allosaurus* grew as big as a dump truck. They hunted alone or in groups of two or three, perhaps stalking herds of plant-eaters until they spotted a weak animal. Other theropods, like *Compsognathus*, were no bigger than a chicken. But they didn't let their size stop them from terrorizing the neighborhood. *Deinonychus* and *Velociraptor* probably hunted in packs to make a meal of an animal more than four times their size.

MEAT-EATERS DON'T NEED FALSE TEETH
With so much munching on flesh and bone, meat-eaters were always breaking or wearing out their teeth. But sharp, new teeth always grew in. You can see some new teeth ready to replace the old ones in this theropod jaw.

KILLER KICK
Deinonychus kicks out at its next victim. The claws on its back feet could slash open an animal's stomach. Its hands, tipped with more claws, would hold the animal down while it bit out a mouthful of flesh. *Deinonychus* may have had feathers, not for flying but to keep warm. Birds evolved from dinosaurs like this one.

HANDS ON

Meat-Eaters Near You

What are the meat-eaters in your neighborhood like? Dogs and cats have some features in common with carnivorous dinosaurs. You can see this particularly in their teeth, legs, and claws.

Many dogs can run fast after their quarry on their long legs. They have sharp, stabbing teeth in the front of their mouth. These are designed to hold their prey down while their back teeth shear and slice the meat into small pieces. The dogs you know probably don't get their food this way, but remember that dogs in the wild, such as wolves, still do.

Cats have similar teeth to dogs, and they use them in much the same way. They also have sharp, curved claws on their paws to grab their prey and then hold on to it. Many dogs' claws are different, because dogs don't use their claws or paws for attack or defense.

Troodon

Daspletosaurus

STEAK-KNIFE TEETH
Carnosaur teeth had curved edges lined with little bumps called serrations. The serrations are clear on the *Troodon* tooth above. The *Daspletosaurus* teeth also have serrations, but they are too small to see.

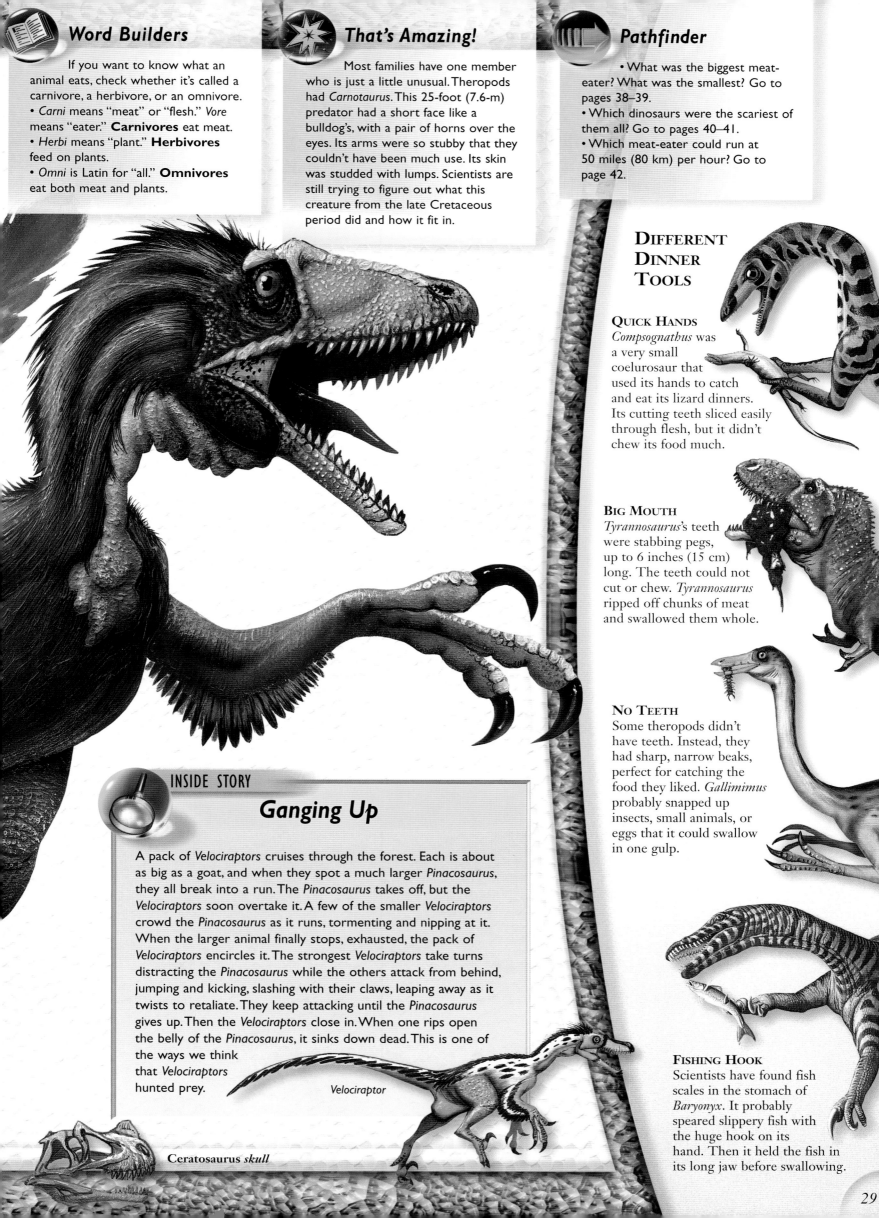

Word Builders

If you want to know what an animal eats, check whether it's called a carnivore, a herbivore, or an omnivore.
• *Carni* means "meat" or "flesh." *Vore* means "eater." **Carnivores** eat meat.
• *Herbi* means "plant." **Herbivores** feed on plants.
• *Omni* is Latin for "all." **Omnivores** eat both meat and plants.

That's Amazing!

Most families have one member who is just a little unusual. Theropods had *Carnotaurus*. This 25-foot (7.6-m) predator had a short face like a bulldog's, with a pair of horns over the eyes. Its arms were so stubby that they couldn't have been much use. Its skin was studded with lumps. Scientists are still trying to figure out what this creature from the late Cretaceous period did and how it fit in.

Pathfinder

• What was the biggest meat-eater? What was the smallest? Go to pages 38–39.
• Which dinosaurs were the scariest of them all? Go to pages 40–41.
• Which meat-eater could run at 50 miles (80 km) per hour? Go to page 42.

DIFFERENT DINNER TOOLS

QUICK HANDS
Compsognathus was a very small coelurosaur that used its hands to catch and eat its lizard dinners. Its cutting teeth sliced easily through flesh, but it didn't chew its food much.

BIG MOUTH
Tyrannosaurus's teeth were stabbing pegs, up to 6 inches (15 cm) long. The teeth could not cut or chew. *Tyrannosaurus* ripped off chunks of meat and swallowed them whole.

NO TEETH
Some theropods didn't have teeth. Instead, they had sharp, narrow beaks, perfect for catching the food they liked. *Gallimimus* probably snapped up insects, small animals, or eggs that it could swallow in one gulp.

FISHING HOOK
Scientists have found fish scales in the stomach of *Baryonyx*. It probably speared slippery fish with the huge hook on its hand. Then it held the fish in its long jaw before swallowing.

INSIDE STORY

Ganging Up

A pack of *Velociraptors* cruises through the forest. Each is about as big as a goat, and when they spot a much larger *Pinacosaurus*, they all break into a run. The *Pinacosaurus* takes off, but the *Velociraptors* soon overtake it. A few of the smaller *Velociraptors* crowd the *Pinacosaurus* as it runs, tormenting and nipping at it. When the larger animal finally stops, exhausted, the pack of *Velociraptors* encircles it. The strongest *Velociraptors* take turns distracting the *Pinacosaurus* while the others attack from behind, jumping and kicking, slashing with their claws, leaping away as it twists to retaliate. They keep attacking until the *Pinacosaurus* gives up. Then the *Velociraptors* close in. When one rips open the belly of the *Pinacosaurus*, it sinks down dead. This is one of the ways we think that *Velociraptors* hunted prey.

Velociraptor

Ceratosaurus *skull*

Conifer pine fossil

Ginkgo fossil

Cycad fossil

The Plant-Eaters

THERE WERE HUNDREDS, probably even thousands, of different plant-eating dinosaurs. In fact, most dinosaurs ate plants rather than meat. It's not easy to survive just on plants because they aren't as nutritious as meat. But in the warm, wet Mesozoic era, plants grew so thickly that dinosaurs had plenty to choose from.

All plant-eaters didn't eat the same things. Their diet depended on what plants they could reach and what their mouths, teeth, and stomachs could handle. Small plant-eaters, such as *Heterodontosaurus* and *Hypsilophodon*, nibbled at low-growing cycads and tree ferns, eating the most nutritious bits—the young leaves and seeds. Hadrosaurs and ceratopsians, such as *Corythosaurus* and *Triceratops*, had rows of teeth and strong chewing muscles. They ground up the tough leaves from cycads and tree ferns, and then let the digestive system do the rest. The huge sauropods, such as *Diplodocus*, stretched their long necks up to the tops of tall conifer trees. They couldn't chew their food, so they swallowed it whole, and then brewed it into a nutritious mixture in their stomachs. All these dinosaurs had the right tools to make the most of the Mesozoic world's plants.

Mouth open   Mouth closed

EATING ACTION
When an ornithopod dinosaur such as *Iguanodon* closed its mouth to chew, the action forced its upper jaw to swing outward. The teeth in the upper jaw and the teeth in the lower jaw then ground against one another. Any food caught in the middle was shredded like a carrot in a grater.

INSIDE STORY

An Earthshaking Fossil Find

Imagine finding the remains of one of the biggest animals ever to walk on Earth. David Gillette, the state paleontologist for Utah, did just that when he discovered *Seismosaurus*. This sauropod was probably 140 feet (42.7 m) long, and it lived 150 million years ago. It was so big that Gillette and his team needed eight years to excavate it. There may still be some bones buried at the site in New Mexico, U.S.A. During the excavation, the team discovered 231 gastroliths, or stomach stones, in the rib cage of the *Seismosaurus*. It had swallowed the stones to help digest food in its stomach. Most of the stones were about the size of a peach, but one was as big as a grapefruit. David Gillette thinks that maybe this larger gastrolith had gotten stuck in the huge creature's throat and caused it to choke to death.

NOSE TO THE GROUND
Two *Stegosaurus* feed on some low-growing ferns. These dinosaurs' front legs were much shorter than their back legs, making it easier to keep their heads down by the food. They had weak teeth, so maybe their narrow snouts picked out only soft things to eat. They didn't chew their food. Instead, they swallowed bundles of plants whole, and broke them down in their large gut. That's why their bodies needed to be so big.

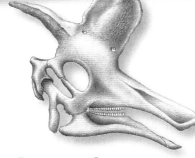

TEETH, MOUTHS, BEAKS

You can tell a lot about a plant-eater and what it ate by the type of teeth it had and the shape of its mouth or beak. All plant-eaters didn't eat the same things or eat in the same way. Some nipped and cut their food. Others grated and ground their food. Still others gulped their food down whole.

SNIP AND SWALLOW
Plateosaurus had small, weak teeth that worked like scissors, snipping off mouthfuls of soft leaves. *Plateosaurus* could not chew. It swallowed food whole.

PLUCK AND GRIND
Lambeosaurus plucked off leaves and fruit with its horny beak, ground them up, and then swallowed. Grinding wore its teeth down, but it had hundreds of replacements.

Word Builders

- *Don* is Latin for "tooth." It's a good word for cracking the code of dinosaur names.
- **Heterodontosaurus** means "lizard with different types of teeth," since the dinosaur had three types of teeth.
- **Iguanodon** means "iguana tooth." The man who discovered *Iguanodon* thought its teeth were like an iguana's.

That's Amazing!

Plant-eating dinosaurs ate cycads, horsetails, ginkgo leaves, conifer needles, ferns, and even flowers. But they couldn't have eaten grass— because there was none to eat! The first grasses didn't grow on Earth until the Eocene epoch, about 25 million years after the last dinosaur had died.

Pathfinder

- What did dinosaur plant food look like? Go to page 13.
- Do you want to see other plant-eaters in armor, like *Stegosaurus*? Go to pages 36–37.
- How long was the longest plant-eating dinosaur ever? How small was the smallest? Go to pages 38–39.

Hadrosaurs had batteries of hundreds of tiny teeth.

STONES IN THEIR STOMACHS
The long-necked sauropods couldn't break up their food with their teeth. So they swallowed stones, called gastroliths, which did the job in their stomachs. The gastroliths moved around, stirring the plants in a dinosaur's stomach, helping the mixture to brew.

NIP AND SLICE
Protoceratops had a parrotlike beak at the front of its mouth for nipping off leaves. Slicing teeth at the back of its mouth then sliced them into a paste.

CUT, STAB, AND CHOP
Heterodontosaurus had three kinds of teeth. It had small cutting teeth at the front of its mouth. Then it had two sets of stabbing, fanglike teeth, and chopping teeth in the back.

STRIP AND SWALLOW
Brachiosaurus had teeth that looked like chisels. It stripped the leaves from tall trees with these teeth but could not chew its food up before swallowing.

The Long Necks

THE LONG-NECKED SAUROPODS were the biggest, heaviest, and longest animals ever to walk Earth. The most massive of them, *Seismosaurus*, grew to 140 feet (42.7 m) long and weighed as much as 10 elephants. No wonder its name means "earthquake lizard."

All the sauropods had incredibly long necks with tiny heads on top. For defense they had long tails, which some could use like whips. In between, their thick, barrel-shaped bodies were held up by four powerful legs. Sauropods such as *Diplodocus* and *Barosaurus* had back legs that were longer than their front legs. They probably reared up onto their hind legs to reach the tasty leaves in the tallest trees, or maybe to scare off predators. *Brachiosaurus*'s front legs were longer than its back legs, helping to lift its long, straight neck even higher into the trees.

The long-necked dinosaurs were at their biggest and most diverse during the Jurassic period. The world was thick with conifer forests and lush ferns for them to eat. Many roamed in small herds to protect their babies and to look for fresh food. These dinosaurs had appetites as big as their bodies, and spent most of the day munching through the tons of food they needed to keep their stomachs full.

THE LONGEST NECK IN THE WORLD
This *Mamenchisaurus* skeleton was found in China and is on display in the capital, Beijing. Its neck was comparatively light because some parts of the bones were as thin as eggshells. This huge fossil needs a metal frame to hold everything in place.

LONG, LONGER, LONGEST
Mamenchisaurus wins the prize, with a 35-foot (10.6-m) long neck that was about half the length of its entire body. With a neck like that, you could easily peek through a fourth-story window. Compared with the sauropods, a giraffe's 7-foot (2-m) neck, with its seven vertebrae, looks a little puny. Sauropods had 12 to 19 neck vertebrae, plus extra pieces of bone for support.

Mamenchisaurus had the longest neck—35 feet (10.6 m)—of any animal we know about.

INSIDE STORY
Dinosaur National Monument

About 150 million years ago, the area was a sandbar. Bodies of dinosaurs washed downriver and stopped there. Now it's Dinosaur National Monument, a big dinosaur graveyard on the border between Utah and Colorado, U.S.A.

There you can see hundreds of bones that belonged to dozens of different dinosaurs, including long-necked sauropods such as *Camarasaurus, Barosaurus, Apatosaurus,* and *Diplodocus.* You can tour the workshops, watch paleontologists prepare fossils, and check out the skeletons and models on display. You can also explore the cliff face that is studded with hundreds of huge bones, and visit a dinosaur graveyard.

A long, whiplike tail balanced the long neck, like a seesaw.

The legs were as straight and strong as columns.

Strong, broad hips held the weight of the body.

The barrel-shaped rib cage protected the internal organs.

Thick shoulder blades fixed the front legs to the body.

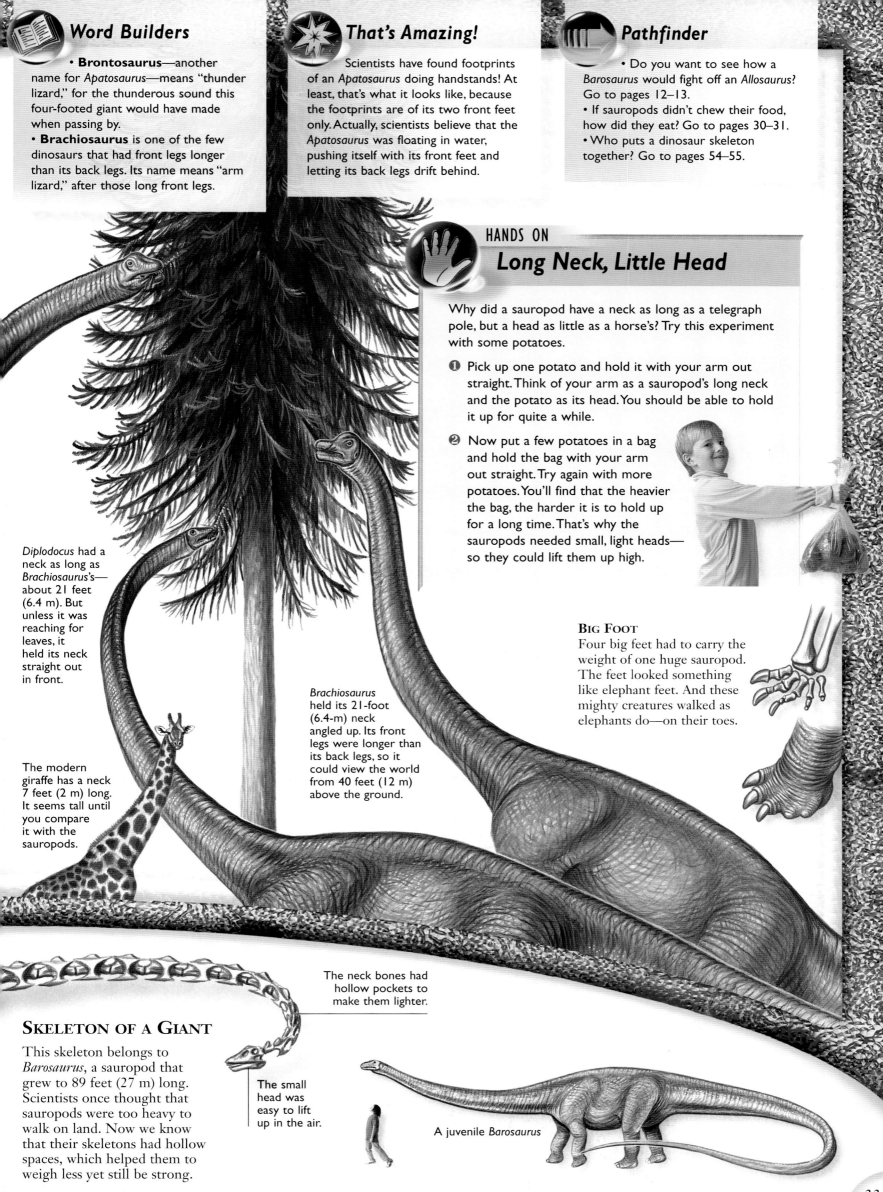

Word Builders

• **Brontosaurus**—another name for *Apatosaurus*—means "thunder lizard," for the thunderous sound this four-footed giant would have made when passing by.
• **Brachiosaurus** is one of the few dinosaurs that had front legs longer than its back legs. Its name means "arm lizard," after those long front legs.

That's Amazing!

Scientists have found footprints of an *Apatosaurus* doing handstands! At least, that's what it looks like, because the footprints are of its two front feet only. Actually, scientists believe that the *Apatosaurus* was floating in water, pushing itself with its front feet and letting its back legs drift behind.

Pathfinder

• Do you want to see how a *Barosaurus* would fight off an *Allosaurus*? Go to pages 12–13.
• If sauropods didn't chew their food, how did they eat? Go to pages 30–31.
• Who puts a dinosaur skeleton together? Go to pages 54–55.

HANDS ON
Long Neck, Little Head

Why did a sauropod have a neck as long as a telegraph pole, but a head as little as a horse's? Try this experiment with some potatoes.

❶ Pick up one potato and hold it with your arm out straight. Think of your arm as a sauropod's long neck and the potato as its head. You should be able to hold it up for quite a while.

❷ Now put a few potatoes in a bag and hold the bag with your arm out straight. Try again with more potatoes. You'll find that the heavier the bag, the harder it is to hold up for a long time. That's why the sauropods needed small, light heads— so they could lift them up high.

Diplodocus had a neck as long as *Brachiosaurus*'s— about 21 feet (6.4 m). But unless it was reaching for leaves, it held its neck straight out in front.

The modern giraffe has a neck 7 feet (2 m) long. It seems tall until you compare it with the sauropods.

Brachiosaurus held its 21-foot (6.4-m) neck angled up. Its front legs were longer than its back legs, so it could view the world from 40 feet (12 m) above the ground.

BIG FOOT
Four big feet had to carry the weight of one huge sauropod. The feet looked something like elephant feet. And these mighty creatures walked as elephants do—on their toes.

The neck bones had hollow pockets to make them lighter.

SKELETON OF A GIANT

This skeleton belongs to *Barosaurus*, a sauropod that grew to 89 feet (27 m) long. Scientists once thought that sauropods were too heavy to walk on land. Now we know that their skeletons had hollow spaces, which helped them to weigh less yet still be strong.

The small head was easy to lift up in the air.

A juvenile *Barosaurus*

The Head Cases

DINOSAURS WERE WEARING some strange headgear toward the end of the Cretaceous period. Some had crests, spikes, prongs, and sacs. They were the hadrosaurs, also called the duck-billed dinosaurs because of their broad, ducklike beaks. They roamed through Asia and North America in herds of up to 10,000 animals, closely related but all looking very different. Some may have used their headgear like trumpets or horns to bellow signals to one another. Perhaps males attracted females with the decorative display. Some may have sniffed out smells with their long nose extensions.

The pachycephalosaurs, or boneheaded dinosaurs, also had unusual headpieces. The very thick domes of solid bone on their skulls were like crash helmets. One idea is that in a fight, a bonehead would charge at its rival and crash head-on. Its thick, bony helmet would protect its tiny brain from damage while it pounded the opponent.

The duckbills walked or ran on two legs but browsed for food on four. The boneheads traveled on two legs. Both duck-billed and boneheaded dinosaurs ate many types of plants, which helped some of the species survive right up to the end of the Age of Dinosaurs.

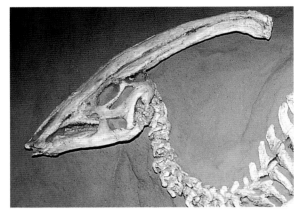

HADROSAUR HEAD
The head crest of *Parasaurolophus* was made of long pieces of hollow bone that reached from its snout over the top of its head. The front of its snout formed a toothless beak, shaped like a duck's bill, for pecking at leaves and fruit.

DOME OF BONE
This *Pachycephalosaurus* skull shows the thick dome of bone that sat like a helmet on the top of this dinosaur's head. Its brain was set deep inside the mass of bone, safe from damage during any clashes with other males. This skull also has some bony spikes down near the nose.

GETTING AHEAD IN THE LATE CRETACEOUS
Different head wear marks out two very different plant-eating dinosaurs. The male *Parasaurolophus* (near right) was a duck-billed dinosaur. Its long, curved head crest was hollow and could honk out a sound like a trombone, perhaps helping it to find a mate or alerting others in the herd to danger. The solid, bony dome of the *Pachycephalosaurus* (far right) may have been for fighting, a tough weapon for head-butting rivals.

Maiasaura

Word Builders

• Dinosaurs get their names for all different reasons. Sometimes, it's because of a particular feature. **Saurolophus** means "lizard crest," for the bony crest on this dinosaur's skull.
• Sometimes, a dinosaur is named in honor of a person or a place. **Edmontosaurus** was named after the Edmonton Formation, a series of rocks near the city of Edmonton, in Canada.

That's Amazing!

How do you tell a male dinosaur from a female? Usually, it's impossible to spot the difference by just looking at their fossilized bones. Scientists need to study their internal organs. Skeletons may provide some clues, however. With *Parasaurolophus*, the female may have been smaller and had a smaller head crest than the male. A male *Tyrannosaurus* had longer bones at the base of its tail than a female.

Pathfinder

• Do you want to see a herd of hadrosaurs on the move? Who traveled with them? Go to pages 14–15.
• What colors were dinosaurs? Go to pages 20–21 and 56.
• How well could dinosaurs hear, see, and smell? Go to pages 42–43.

INSIDE STORY

On the Move with the Hadrosaurs

There's a whole lot of hooting and honking going on! A hadrosaur herd at mating time was probably a loud, colorful scene. Imagine two or more species of thousands of animals living and traveling together—thousands of *Parasaurolophus* and *Lambeosaurus*, for example, as far as the eye can see.

You can spot the male *Parasaurolophus* because they have very long, curved crests. The females' crests are shorter, while the infants have no crests at all. The *Lambeosaurus* are the dinosaurs with the crests that look like hatchets with a spike at the back.

In the noisy crowd, each animal calls out to keep from getting lost. Different crest shapes produce different sounds, and each individual dinosaur has its own particular voice. At mating time, the calls get louder and fiercer as the males compete with one another, trumpeting to impress the females. The males' crests might even take on a rainbow display of color as they parade about, as birds do today.

Infant
Parasaurolophus

Female
Parasaurolophus

Cross section of male *Parasaurolophus* crest

Prenocephale   Stygimoloch

HEADGEAR

CREST AND SPIKE
Lambeosaurus had a hollow, flat crest on top of its head. A long, narrow spike sat behind the crest, pointing backward.

SOUND SAC
Edmontosaurus was a flatheaded hadrosaur with no fancy head-gear. But it may have inflated a sac of skin on the front of its face to make sounds.

SPIKE AND SAC
Saurolophus had a head spike and possibly also an inflatable nose sac. By blowing air into this sac, it may have called to others.

DOME AND STUDS
Stegoceras was a bonehead. Its dome of solid bone was circled by a frill of bony studs.

The Armored Division

SOME PLANT-EATING DINOSAURS were built to stand and fight off an attacker. They were armed with spikes and horns, and protected by plates and shields. This array of weaponry helped them defend themselves, but the armor was heavy and prevented a quick getaway.

Stegosaurs had bony plates sticking out along their backs, and spikes at the end of their tails. The plates on *Stegosaurus* were like big triangles. The plates on *Kentrosaurus* were thinner, but it had spikes all along its tail. It may have had shoulder spikes, too. These slow-moving creatures were most common in the late Jurassic period.

Ankylosaurs appeared at the same time as stegosaurs and lived well into the Cretaceous period. With their coats of bony armor across their backs, they were like moving tanks. Spikes poked out along their shoulders and sides. Some, such as *Euoplocephalus*, also had heavy tail clubs.

The ceratopsians were the horned dinosaurs. Their heads were built for a frontal attack, with a variety of nose and brow horns, and collars of bone around the neck. The ceratopsians were late arrivals to the Cretaceous world, spreading in vast herds across North America and Asia. Some were around at the time of the dinosaur extinction.

FOSSIL FRILL
This fossil skeleton of *Triceratops* shows its frill of solid bone. The frill covered the soft neck of *Triceratops*, protecting it from attack. The two horns above its eyes could grow longer than 3 feet (1 m). The third horn on its nose was stumplike.

CHARGE!
An angry *Triceratops* on the attack would have been an awesome sight. Think of a charging rhinoceros, double in size, and you'll begin to get the idea. Hungry meat-eaters weren't the only dinosaurs that had to beware those lethal horns. Damage found on the skulls of some *Triceratops* shows that they probably used their horns when battling for a mate.

 INSIDE STORY

The Big Dig

One of the biggest dinosaur digs took place in the rock beds near the village of Tendaguru in Tanzania, Africa. Dinosaur bones were first reported in the area by a German mining engineer in 1907. Soon afterward, the Natural History Museum in Berlin, Germany, organized an excavation that lasted for five years. At its peak, more than 500 people were digging for bones and carrying them through the jungle on the four-day march to the coast. More than 250 tons of rocks and fossils were dug up, carted away, and shipped to Germany. Among the bones were skeletons of the huge *Brachiosaurus*, the stegosaur *Kentrosaurus*, and the swift, plant-eating *Dryosaurus*.

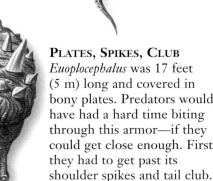

SOME DINOSAUR HARDWARE

PLATES, SPIKES, CLUB
Euoplocephalus was 17 feet (5 m) long and covered in bony plates. Predators would have had a hard time biting through this armor—if they could get close enough. First they had to get past its shoulder spikes and tail club.

SCOOTING *SCUTELLOSAURUS*
Scutellosaurus was one of the earliest armored dinosaurs. The armor covering its body had rows of bony lumps called scutes. This dinosaur was light, so it could run from trouble on its two back legs.

Word Builders

• **Stegosaurus** means "roofed lizard." The scientists that found *Stegosaurus* thought at first that its plates lay flat along its back, like roof tiles, instead of standing upright.
• *Keratos* means "horn," and *ops* means "face" in ancient Greek. Join them together for **ceratopsian,** or "horned face." Add *tri*, which means "three," and you get **Triceratops,** the "three-horned-face" dinosaur.

That's Amazing!

• In Alberta, Canada, there is a mass grave of ceratopsians. Scientists think they tried to cross a river and drowned, just as buffaloes have sometimes done.
• In the Rockies, fossils of a herd of up to 10,000 *Maiasaura* have been found. They may have been wiped out by poisonous gas released from a volcano.

Pathfinder

• What happened to dinosaurs, such as *Triceratops*, during the mass extinction? Go to pages 58–59.
• How did *Stegosaurus* use its back plates to help it warm up or cool down? Go to page 19.
• Do you want to see a dinosaur with a tail club in action? Go to pages 20–21.

HANDS ON
Make a Dinosaur Mobile

1 Choose six big dinosaurs from this book. Trace or draw their outlines onto a sheet of cardboard.

2 Cut out each shape and color both sides. Punch a hole in the top center of each dinosaur.

3 Cut six different lengths of string. Thread a string through the hole in each dinosaur and tie it. With the other ends of the strings, tie three dinosaurs to one stick and the other three dinosaurs to a second stick.

4 Use two more strings to tie the two sticks to a third stick.

5 Hang up your mobile.

SPIKED *STEGOSAURUS*
Stegosaurus, which reached a length of 30 feet (9 m), used its tail spikes to swipe at and stab attackers. The plates of bone along its back were probably not for defense, but instead helped it to keep warm or cool.

SHIELDED *SAUROPELTA*
This was a 19-foot (5.8-m) nodosaur, a type of ankylosaur. Its bony back shield, lined with cones and studs, and its shoulder spikes gave it good protection, especially if it hunkered down to cover its soft underbelly.

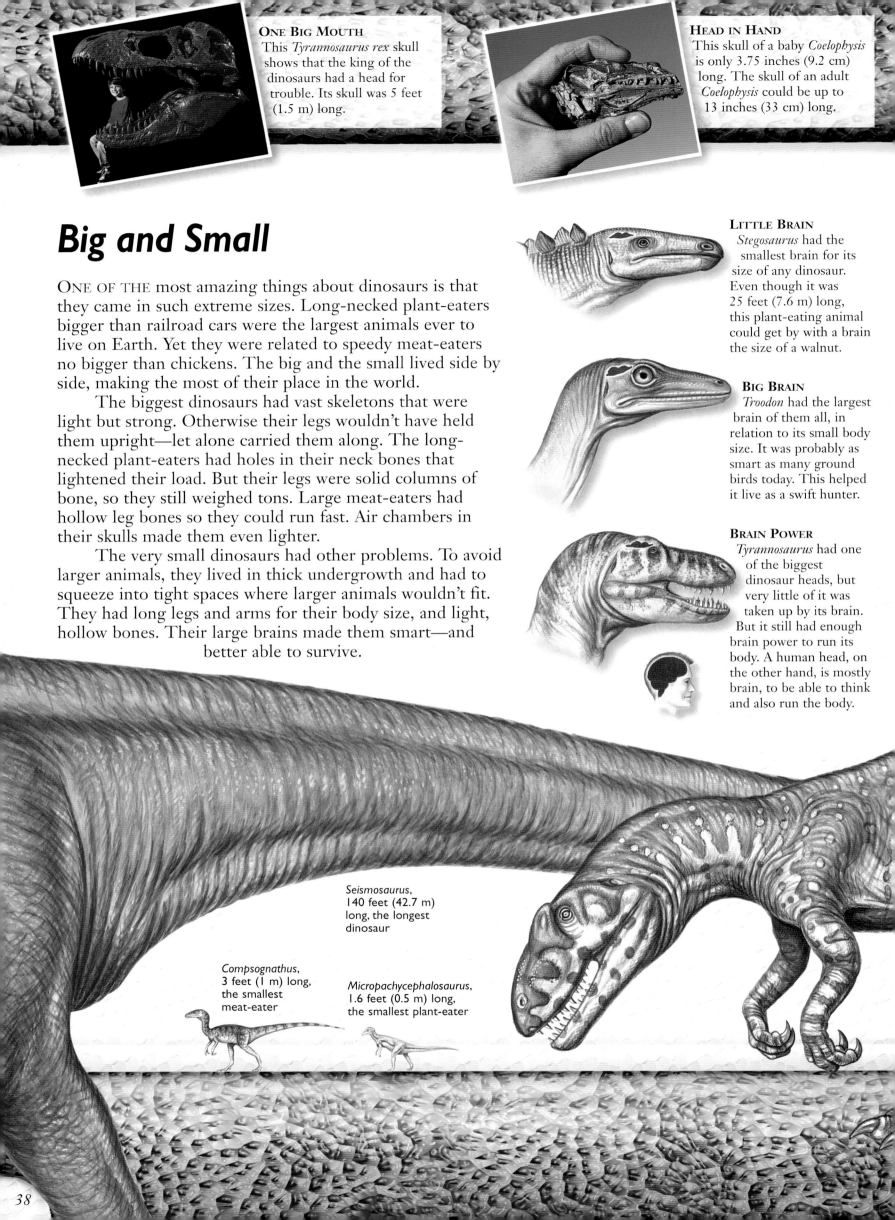

Big and Small

ONE OF THE most amazing things about dinosaurs is that they came in such extreme sizes. Long-necked plant-eaters bigger than railroad cars were the largest animals ever to live on Earth. Yet they were related to speedy meat-eaters no bigger than chickens. The big and the small lived side by side, making the most of their place in the world.

The biggest dinosaurs had vast skeletons that were light but strong. Otherwise their legs wouldn't have held them upright—let alone carried them along. The long-necked plant-eaters had holes in their neck bones that lightened their load. But their legs were solid columns of bone, so they still weighed tons. Large meat-eaters had hollow leg bones so they could run fast. Air chambers in their skulls made them even lighter.

The very small dinosaurs had other problems. To avoid larger animals, they lived in thick undergrowth and had to squeeze into tight spaces where larger animals wouldn't fit. They had long legs and arms for their body size, and light, hollow bones. Their large brains made them smart—and better able to survive.

LITTLE BRAIN
Stegosaurus had the smallest brain for its size of any dinosaur. Even though it was 25 feet (7.6 m) long, this plant-eating animal could get by with a brain the size of a walnut.

BIG BRAIN
Troodon had the largest brain of them all, in relation to its small body size. It was probably as smart as many ground birds today. This helped it live as a swift hunter.

BRAIN POWER
Tyrannosaurus had one of the biggest dinosaur heads, but very little of it was taken up by its brain. But it still had enough brain power to run its body. A human head, on the other hand, is mostly brain, to be able to think and also run the body.

Seismosaurus, 140 feet (42.7 m) long, the longest dinosaur

Compsognathus, 3 feet (1 m) long, the smallest meat-eater

Micropachycephalosaurus, 1.6 feet (0.5 m) long, the smallest plant-eater

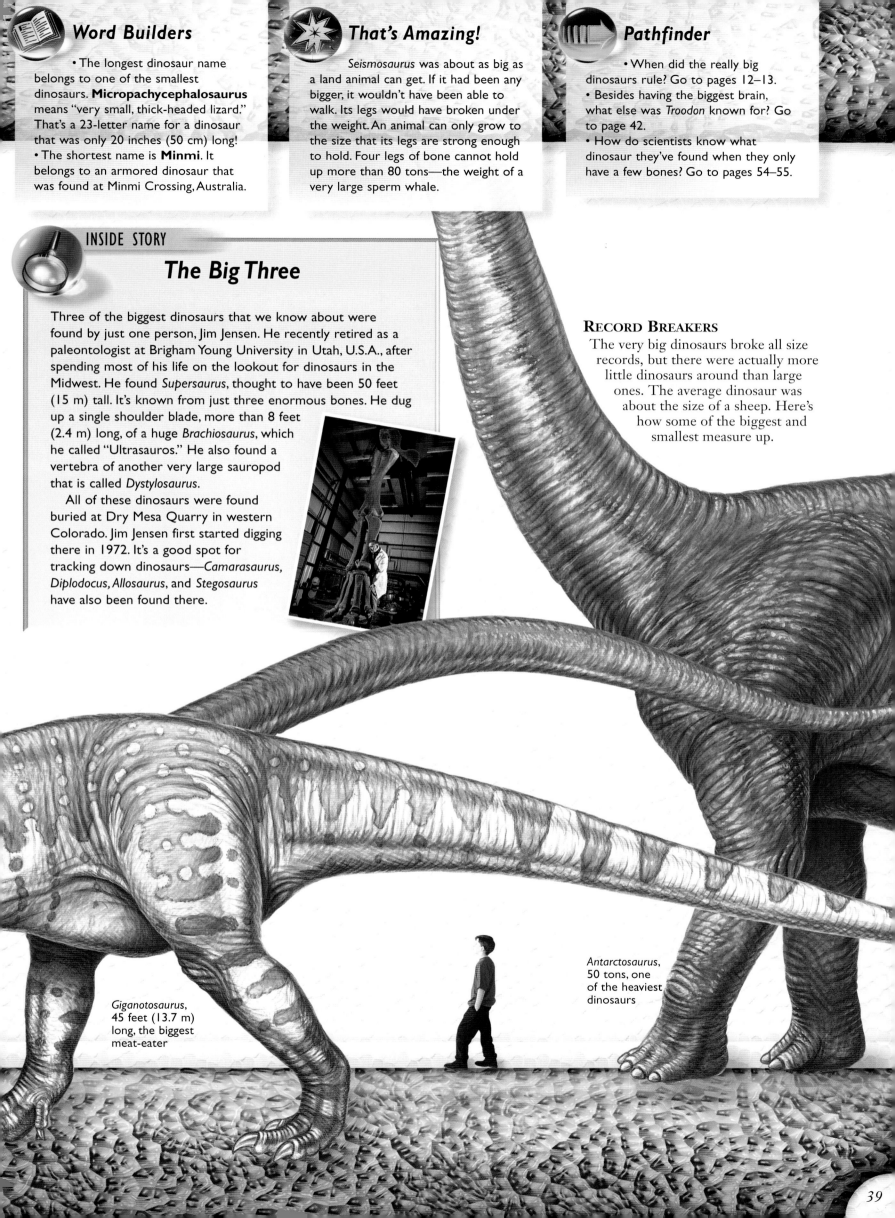

Word Builders

• The longest dinosaur name belongs to one of the smallest dinosaurs. **Micropachycephalosaurus** means "very small, thick-headed lizard." That's a 23-letter name for a dinosaur that was only 20 inches (50 cm) long!
• The shortest name is **Minmi**. It belongs to an armored dinosaur that was found at Minmi Crossing, Australia.

That's Amazing!

Seismosaurus was about as big as a land animal can get. If it had been any bigger, it wouldn't have been able to walk. Its legs would have broken under the weight. An animal can only grow to the size that its legs are strong enough to hold. Four legs of bone cannot hold up more than 80 tons—the weight of a very large sperm whale.

Pathfinder

• When did the really big dinosaurs rule? Go to pages 12–13.
• Besides having the biggest brain, what else was *Troodon* known for? Go to page 42.
• How do scientists know what dinosaur they've found when they only have a few bones? Go to pages 54–55.

INSIDE STORY

The Big Three

Three of the biggest dinosaurs that we know about were found by just one person, Jim Jensen. He recently retired as a paleontologist at Brigham Young University in Utah, U.S.A., after spending most of his life on the lookout for dinosaurs in the Midwest. He found *Supersaurus*, thought to have been 50 feet (15 m) tall. It's known from just three enormous bones. He dug up a single shoulder blade, more than 8 feet (2.4 m) long, of a huge *Brachiosaurus*, which he called "Ultrasauros." He also found a vertebra of another very large sauropod that is called *Dystylosaurus*.

All of these dinosaurs were found buried at Dry Mesa Quarry in western Colorado. Jim Jensen first started digging there in 1972. It's a good spot for tracking down dinosaurs—*Camarasaurus*, *Diplodocus*, *Allosaurus*, and *Stegosaurus* have also been found there.

RECORD BREAKERS

The very big dinosaurs broke all size records, but there were actually more little dinosaurs around than large ones. The average dinosaur was about the size of a sheep. Here's how some of the biggest and smallest measure up.

Giganotosaurus, 45 feet (13.7 m) long, the biggest meat-eater

Antarctosaurus, 50 tons, one of the heaviest dinosaurs

The Tough Guys

THE FIERCEST OF all the dinosaurs were the large, meat-eating theropods. They stood at the top of the food chain in the Mesozoic world, and they ate whatever came their way. They were huge in size. Some of them could grow to more than 30 feet (10 m) long—bigger than a dump truck. Their heads could be as long as a child's body, and each tooth could grow as big as a carving knife.

Big theropods first evolved during the Jurassic period. The carnivore that wore the "king of the dinosaurs" crown changed over time and from continent to continent. To start, *Allosaurus* ruled the late Jurassic world. But as the Cretaceous period dawned, *Carcharodontosaurus* took over in Africa, followed by *Spinosaurus*. North America was the domain of *Acrocanthosaurus* in the early Cretaceous period. Then *Albertosaurus* and *Tyrannosaurus* took the lead. South America saw the arrival of possibly the biggest meat-eater of all, *Giganotosaurus*, at the end of the Age of Dinosaurs.

Then there were the "princes of the dinosaurs," much smaller but equally fierce dromaeosaurs such as *Velociraptor*, *Deinonychus*, and *Dromaeosaurus*. Fast and smart, they probably hunted in packs, jumping on larger animals or terrorizing smaller ones. The sickle claws on their feet were the lethal weapons of these tough guys.

LARGE AND LIGHT
This *Allosaurus* skeleton is typical of the big theropods. Its skull was light but strong. Powerful legs held up its solid body. Some theropods had stubby arms that couldn't do much, but *Allosaurus* had arms that worked like grappling hooks.

INSIDE STORY

A Dinosaur Called Sue

Sue is the most complete *Tyrannosaurus rex* skeleton in the world—and the most expensive. She was found in 1990 in South Dakota, U.S.A., but then a fight started over who actually owned her. Did she belong to the team of paleontologists who found her? Or to the farmer who managed the area where she was found? Or to the federal government, which owned the land? Different states and countries have different laws about who owns a fossil after it is found. In some places, fossils belong to the person who owns the land where the fossils were actually discovered. In other places, the fossils belong to the finder or to the government.

A court finally decided that Sue belonged to the farmer, and he sold her at an auction. She was bought by the Field Museum in Chicago for $8.3 million. There she will be looked after properly, where scientists can study her and the public can see her.

TERRIBLE CLAW
What *Deinonychus* lacked in its 10-foot (3-m) size, it made up for with a lethal killing claw, 5 inches (13 cm) long. The claw was attached to the second toe of each foot, where it swiveled up and down. When *Deinonychus* attacked an animal, it kicked its leg out. The claw would first stab through flesh and then swivel, slashing a long, fatal gash in its prey.

Deinonychus *hand*   Deinocheirus *hand*

Tyrant is the name given to a harsh ruler, which is why **Tyrannosaurus** got the name meaning "tyrant lizard." Sometimes it is called **Tyrannosaurus rex**. Because *rex* is Latin for "king," this name means "king of the tyrant lizards." **Tyrannosaurus** is the name of the genus that this dinosaur belongs to, while **rex** is the name of its species. Every dinosaur has a genus name and a species name.

• What was it like during the Jurassic and the Cretaceous periods? Go to pages 12–15.
• What did meat-eaters' teeth look like? Go to page 28.
• How fast could big predators run? Go to page 43.

KILLER SKULLS

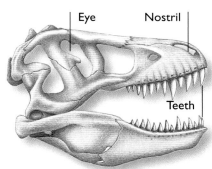

Eye   Nostril

Teeth

EXTRA WIDE
The skull of *Tyrannosaurus* had to be strong to crunch down on and kill its prey. Its heavy jaw had an extra joint in the middle, so the mouth could open wider to take extra-large bites. It had bony bits above and below its eyes to make sure they weren't poked out by struggling prey.

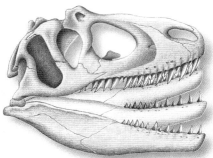

BITE ACTION
Allosaurus's skull was 3 feet (1 m) long. The powerful head was kept light by big holes at the front and back of the skull. Its jaw could open wide to bite and slide through flesh. Here, the jaw opens and closes to show its bite action.

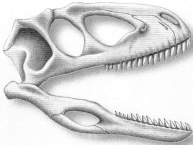

LIGHT BITE
Deinonychus was a smaller meat-eater, but it could still deliver a ferocious bite with its wide, gaping mouth. Dozens of small, curved teeth acted like a saw to cut through muscles and skin.

HEAD-ON
Tyrannosaurus weighed as much as a killer whale but was twice the size and built for head-on attack. *Tyrannosaurus* could see what was happening on all sides, even when it was looking straight ahead. *Tyrannosaurus* could see, in perfect three-dimensional vision, whatever lay directly in front of it. After powerful back legs pushed *Tyrannosaurus* forward, its huge mouth could gape wide to crunch down with more than 50 stabbing teeth.

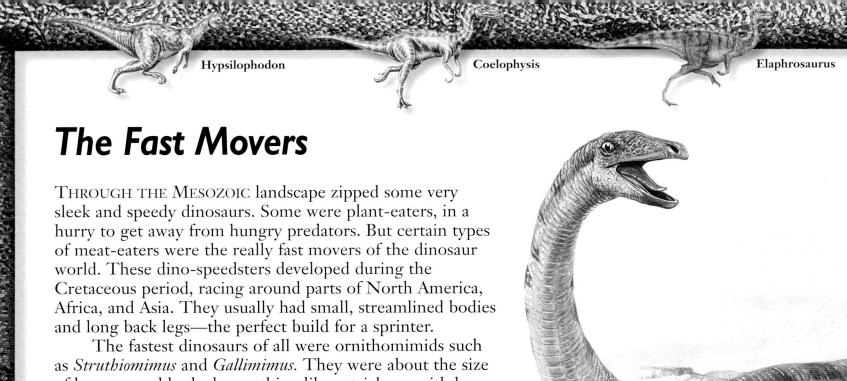

The Fast Movers

THROUGH THE MESOZOIC landscape zipped some very sleek and speedy dinosaurs. Some were plant-eaters, in a hurry to get away from hungry predators. But certain types of meat-eaters were the really fast movers of the dinosaur world. These dino-speedsters developed during the Cretaceous period, racing around parts of North America, Africa, and Asia. They usually had small, streamlined bodies and long back legs—the perfect build for a sprinter.

The fastest dinosaurs of all were ornithomimids such as *Struthiomimus* and *Gallimimus*. They were about the size of humans and looked something like ostriches—with long, gangly arms and legs, and small, toothless heads. They probably fed on insects or small mammals and lizards. They ran at up to 40 miles (64 km) per hour to escape larger, more powerful predators.

The troodontids were fast—but not that fast. They were smaller, too, and not quite so birdlike. But they were some of the smartest dinosaurs. Their large eyes would spot small animals, and then they'd use speed and agility to dash after their dinner. They had many small teeth and a sickle claw, which probably worked like a stabbing weapon. They were the pursuit predators of the prehistoric world.

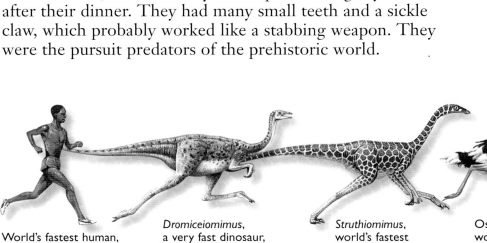

World's fastest human, 22.8 mph (36.5 km/h)

Dromiceiomimus, a very fast dinosaur, 30 mph (48 km/h)

Struthiomimus, world's fastest dinosaur, 40 mph (64 km/h)

Ostrich, world's fastest running bird, 50 mph (80 km/h)

THE WORLD RECORD HOLDERS
In a race, the ornithomimids would have left humans far behind. *Struthiomimus* could have topped 40 miles (64 km) per hour, almost twice as fast as the fastest human in the world. Only a few modern animals, such as the ostrich, could run faster than a speeding ornithomimid.

DINOSAUR SENSES

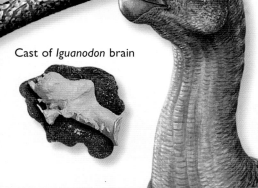

Cast of *Iguanodon* brain

TASTING AND SMELLING
The front part of *Iguanodon*'s brain—that part of the brain that did the tasting and smelling work—was well developed. This plant-eater had a good sense of smell and taste, so it might have sniffed out hidden predators or distant plants.

SEEING
It's not easy to find out from a pile of fossils what dinosaurs could see. But certain dinosaurs' skeletons give scientists some clues. For example, *Troodon* had large eye sockets for its big eyes, and a large part of its brain was devoted to seeing. So it probably had a good sense of sight, and may have seen in the dark.

Word Builders

• *Mimos* is the Greek word for mimic, which means "to look like or resemble." *Ornitho* means "bird," so the **ornithomimids** were "bird mimics."
• *Struthio* is the Latin name for "ostrich," which makes **Struthiomimus** an "ostrich mimic."
• *Gallus* is the Latin name for "chicken." **Gallimimus** is a "chicken mimic."

That's Amazing!

How fast could big predators run? Not very quickly, scientists think. The faster they ran, the more they could injure themselves. If a 6-ton *Tyrannosaurus* tripped while running more than 9–12 miles (15–20 km) per hour, it would have crushed its head and rib cage when it fell. So the big meat-eaters probably lumbered along at an earth-shuddering fast walk.

Pathfinder

• Why could dinosaurs move around better than most other animals that lived during the Mesozoic era? Go to pages 16–17.
• *Gallimimus* and *Albertosaurus* were both meat-eaters. What other meat-eaters were there? Go to pages 28–29.
• How does a footprint turn into a fossil in rock? Go to pages 48–49.

CAN'T CATCH *GALLIMIMUS*

When fleet-footed *Gallimimus* got going, there was no way a lumbering *Albertosaurus* could catch it. *Gallimimus* could tear along at speeds of up to 30 miles (48 km) per hour. It could also change direction suddenly, dodging and weaving out of *Albertosaurus*'s reach. At over 6 feet (2 m) tall and 17 feet (5 m) long, *Gallimimus* was the biggest ornithomimid. But its slender frame made it seem much smaller than it really was.

INSIDE STORY

Follow Those Feet

Fossilized footprints can reveal much about an extinct animal. As well as showing how big its feet were and how long its stride was, a set of footprints can tell you how fast the animal traveled. The faster it ran, the farther apart its footprints were.

A leading expert on dinosaur footprints, James Farlow is a paleontologist at Indiana–Purdue University, in the U.S.A. He has studied footprints of birds such as emus. From them, he's been able to estimate the speeds of several dinosaurs that left footprints in Texas. One Jurassic carnivore ran at 26.5 miles (42.8 km) per hour, while sauropods Farlow has studied ambled about at 1–2 miles (2–3 km) per hour.

HEARING

Most hadrosaurs, such as *Saurolophus*, had special headgear for making sounds. But sound would have been useful only if they also had a good sense of hearing so they could make out what other hadrosaurs in the herd were honking back at them.

TOUCHING

Touch is the toughest sense of all for scientists to understand about an extinct animal. But with its thick, scaly skin, a dinosaur's sense of touch must have been very different from ours.

The Dinosaur Puzzle

Dinosaurs are a big mystery because they've been dead for so long. Here is your chance to see how scientists have put together the puzzle of the dinosaurs by following the pieces back in time. The fossil evidence dinosaurs left behind is the place to start. Glimpse some famous fossil finds before visiting an excavation site. Then head to the laboratory to see a dinosaur being brought back to life. Your journey finishes with the big mystery of why all dinosaurs died—even though some of their relatives are still alive today.

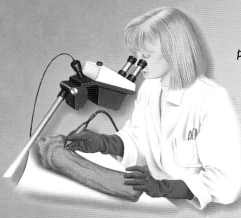

Snakefly fossil

Fish skeleton fossil

Fossil Evidence

EVERYTHING WE KNOW about dinosaurs has come from the study of their fossils. But not even one in every thousand dinosaurs that walked Earth left bits of fossil evidence behind. That's because conditions have to be just right for an animal to turn into a fossil. First, the animal has to die in the right place, by a river or a lake. Then a flood might hit, and its body might get washed into the water, to be buried by mud and sand, and eventually preserved as a fossil.

Usually the hard parts—the bones and teeth—are preserved. The soft bits, like the flesh and guts, tend to rot or get eaten by scavengers. So most fossils are bones and teeth. Sometimes paleontologists turn up some footprints, eggs, and dung. Occasionally, a dinosaur was mummified by fine grit, so the fossil has impressions of dinosaur skin.

Fossils are found in sandstone, mudstone, shale, and limestone—rocks that started out as sediment in rivers and lakes. There are some places on Earth where these types of rocks are packed full of dinosaur fossils. Dinosaur bones from throughout the Mesozoic era have been found since the 1870s in the midwestern United States and Canada. Parts of China, Mongolia, Africa, and South America are also good hunting grounds for dinosaur evidence.

INSIDE STORY
A Dinosaur Bone Park

Dinosaur Provincial Park is a slice of the dinosaur world preserved in fossil form. It is located in the badlands of Alberta, in Canada, on the Red Deer River. This river has cut deep ravines into the Canadian prairie and the surrounding rock to expose the final resting place of countless Cretaceous dinosaurs.

If you visit the park, you can walk along trails that pass right through these erosion gullies and see dinosaur fossils still stuck in the rock. The landscape has been weathered into mysterious formations, called hoodoos, which look like soldiers standing guard. You can also visit the Royal Tyrrell Museum Field Station at the site. It has displays that recreate the late Cretaceous world and show some of the spectacular skeleton fossils that have been excavated in the park.

HOW A DINOSAUR FOSSIL IS FORMED

BODY OUT OF REACH
After a dinosaur died, its carcass was washed into a river. Its flesh rotted or was eaten, and only the skeleton remained.

SKELETON COVER-UP
The skeleton was buried under layers of sand or mud. This protected it from further decay or from being washed away.

Word Builders

• The word **fossil** comes from the Latin *fossilis*, meaning "dug up."
• A word for stone is *lithos*. So **gastroliths** are "stomach stones," while the "study of stones" is known as **lithology**. *Ology* means "study of."
• *Geo* means "Earth." So **geology** is the word for the "study of Earth."

That's Amazing!

Scientists estimate that for every 100 different living things that have ever existed on Earth, 95 of them are now extinct. Of all the animals and plants that are extinct, only a small proportion have been preserved as fossils. So we will never know anything at all about most of the plants and animals that have lived on Earth.

Pathfinder

• Is a pliosaur a type of dinosaur? Go to pages 24–25.
• What dinosaurs used to live in the area that is now the Gobi Desert? Go to pages 15 and 50.
• How do paleontologists remove dinosaur fossils from the ground? Go to pages 52–53.

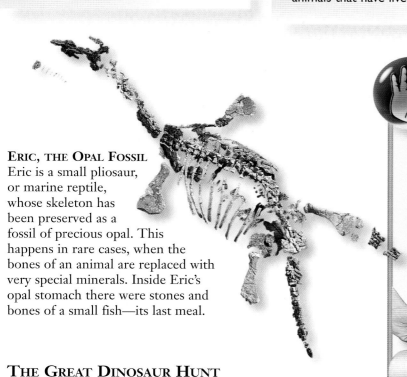

ERIC, THE OPAL FOSSIL

Eric is a small pliosaur, or marine reptile, whose skeleton has been preserved as a fossil of precious opal. This happens in rare cases, when the bones of an animal are replaced with very special minerals. Inside Eric's opal stomach there were stones and bones of a small fish—its last meal.

THE GREAT DINOSAUR HUNT

Two paleontologists search for dinosaur fossils in one of the most important places for dinosaur finds in the world—the Gobi Desert in Mongolia. There are probably countless dinosaur fossils buried all over the world, but the only way to know they are there is if a part of a fossil has been exposed by the wind or rain. To find a dinosaur fossil, paleontologists need skill, dedication, and a lot of luck.

HANDS ON

Fossil Making

You can make your own modern-day fossils. You will need a shallow box or dish, modeling clay, plaster of paris, water, and a spoon. You'll also need some shells, leaves, or anything else that might make a fossil.

① Fill the box or dish with a flat layer of clay.

② Press the shells or leaves into the clay to make an impression. Then remove them.

③ Mix 6 cups plaster of paris with 4 cups water. Pour the mixture onto the clay. Leave it until it sets hard.

④ Carefully separate the plaster from the clay. The plaster and the clay are like the ancient life form and its imprint in the rock. The imprint in the rock is known as the mold. A life form that has turned to stone is called the cast.

BONES INTO FOSSILS
The river sediments turned to rock over time. The bones were replaced by minerals to form fossils, hard like rock.

FOSSILS BACK ON TOP
Movements inside Earth lifted up the rock and brought the fossil close to Earth's surface. Erosion exposed the fossil.

Following Fossil Clues

FOSSIL TEETH AND bones do more than give us clues about what dinosaurs looked like. These fossils also tell us about how dinosaurs lived. Dinosaur bones that fractured and healed again, and bones with arthritis and tumors, show some injuries and illnesses that dinosaurs suffered. Bones with gnaw marks or bite marks can reveal what creature killed a dinosaur or scavenged on its carcass. We can find out even more about the killer from the teeth that are often scattered around fossil skeletons, because predators' teeth fell out as they chomped and chewed on their prey.

But dinosaurs left behind other fossil clues, too. Fossilized dung reveals what dinosaurs ate as well as how they ate it—whether they chewed prey or plants into pieces or swallowed them whole. Dinosaur footprints in rocks show how fast or slowly they moved. From their tracks, we also know that some traveled in vast herds, while others lived alone. Their skin impressions show that they were protected by a tough outer layer. And from their nests and eggs, we know how dinosaurs took care of their babies, living together to bring up the next generation. With these clues, we can create a picture of dinosaurs and their world.

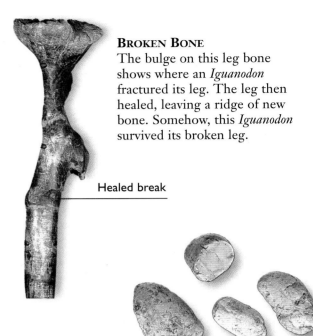

BROKEN BONE
The bulge on this leg bone shows where an *Iguanodon* fractured its leg. The leg then healed, leaving a ridge of new bone. Somehow, this *Iguanodon* survived its broken leg.

Healed break

DINO DUNG
Sometimes, dinosaur droppings turned into fossils as hard as rock, called coprolites. Coprolites come in all shapes and sizes and can contain bits and pieces of seeds, pinecones, plant stems, and even crushed bones. Scientists study dino dung to learn what dinosaurs ate and how they ate it.

INSIDE STORY

Stampede

At Lark Quarry in Australia, there are hundreds of dinosaur footprints, fossilized in a minute of action. Paleontologists have studied the footprints and have a good idea of what happened there millions of years ago. Dozens of small meat-eaters

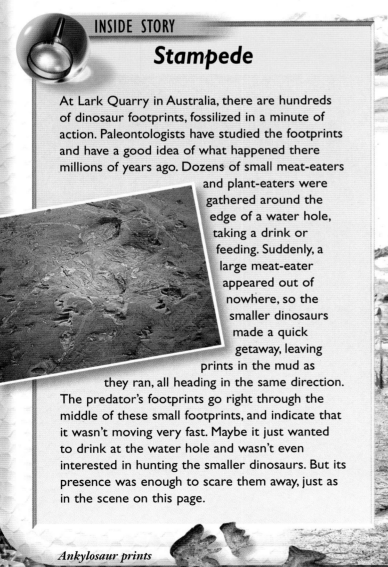

and plant-eaters were gathered around the edge of a water hole, taking a drink or feeding. Suddenly, a large meat-eater appeared out of nowhere, so the smaller dinosaurs made a quick getaway, leaving prints in the mud as they ran, all heading in the same direction. The predator's footprints go right through the middle of these small footprints, and indicate that it wasn't moving very fast. Maybe it just wanted to drink at the water hole and wasn't even interested in hunting the smaller dinosaurs. But its presence was enough to scare them away, just as in the scene on this page.

STUCK IN THE MUD
A few minutes ago, these small plant-eaters and meat-eaters were minding their own business, having a drink in the river. But the minute they sense a meat-eating predator, they make a run for it, leaving their footprints behind in the soft mud. The riverbank is soon covered in a mess of muddy prints. It is the perfect place for prints to be preserved as fossils.

Ankylosaur prints

Prosauropod prints

Word Builders

• Lite comes from *lithos*, which means "stone." *Copro* means "dung," so **coprolite** means "dung stone."
• *Ichnos* means "footprint," and an **ichnite** is the technical name for a "footprint fossil."
• Fossil eggs are called **oolites**, because *oo* means "egg."

That's Amazing!

The largest known dinosaur doesn't have a name. We know about it only because it left some footprints near Broome, in Australia, where there are many dinosaur footprints. Some of them, over 3 feet (1 m) round, may have belonged to a sauropod that was even bigger than *Seismosaurus* or "Ultrasauros."

Pathfinder

• Why did some dinosaurs live in groups and herds, while others lived by themselves? Go to pages 20–21.
• How did dinosaurs build nests? Go to pages 22–23.
• What does dinosaur skin look like? Go to page 43.

HANDS ON
Make Tyrannosaurus Feet Move

❶ Trace the *Tyrannosaurus* footprint opposite onto a piece of paper. Ask an adult to help you enlarge this so the footprint is 3 feet (1 m) long. Now trace the enlarged footprint twice, onto two pieces of cardboard. Cut out the two footprints.

❷ Take your footprints outside for some *Tyrannosaurus* traveling. Lay the two footprints 20 feet (6 m) apart, one in front of the other. That would be the distance between the footprints if *Tyrannosaurus* were walking through your yard. Have the dinosaur run by laying the footprints 40 feet (12 m) apart. How many steps do you need to take to match a *Tyrannosaurus* when it's walking? Running?

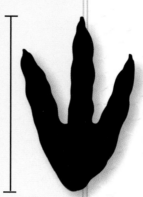

3 feet (1 m)

MAKING TRACKS

Hadrosaur prints

COELUROSAUR PRINTS
Most small meat-eaters left footprints that looked a lot like birds' footprints with slender toe marks. They were much smaller than the large meat-eaters' footprints.

CARNOSAUR PRINTS
Large meat-eaters walked on their two back feet, each of which had three large toes. Some of their footprints even show the clear imprint of the claw on the end of each toe.

SAUROPOD PRINTS
The big sauropods walked around on four feet. Their back feet made huge footprints that were almost circular. Their front feet made smaller, U-shaped prints.

CERATOPSIAN PRINTS
The ceratopsians traveled on all fours. Their smaller front prints were farther out than their larger, four-toed back prints because they walked with their front legs a little farther apart.

Foot bones   *Hand bones*

Famous Finds

FOR THOUSANDS OF years, people dug up oversized bones, but they couldn't work out what they were. No one could imagine creatures being so huge and so different from all the animals they knew. Then, in the 1820s, Gideon Mantell realized that the big fossil teeth and bones he had collected came from a gigantic creature that no longer existed. He thought it had been a reptile, and called it *Iguanodon*.

From then on, people became more and more fascinated with dinosaurs. New discoveries of large bones caused a big stir, even though it wasn't until 1858 that the first almost-complete dinosaur skeleton was found—a *Hadrosaurus*, near Haddonfield, New Jersey, U.S.A. In 1878, the skeletons of 24 *Iguanodons* were found by coal miners near the town of Bernissart, in Belgium. This was the first opportunity to study many complete dinosaurs.

With more dinosaur discoveries, knowledge about them kept on growing. There was even a dinosaur rush at the end of the 19th century, when new American sites like Bone Cabin and Como Bluff revealed many huge dinosaurs, such as *Apatosaurus*, *Diplodocus*, and *Barosaurus*. Expeditions to Africa and Asia in the first half of the 20th century uncovered more fabulous treasure troves of fossils. The quest for dinosaurs continues today, on all continents.

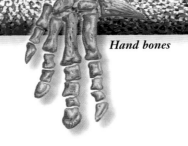

CALL THEM DINOSAURS
Sir Richard Owen was a great English paleontologist and is called the father of the dinosaurs. In 1842, he realized that several large fossilized reptiles all belonged to the same extinct group of animals. He called them Dinosauria. He also described many new dinosaurs, including the sauropod *Cetiosaurus* and the armored *Scelidosaurus*.

DOWN IN THE SWAMP
A swamp becomes the final resting place for dozens of *Iguanodons*— perhaps an *Iguanodon* graveyard, like elephant graveyards in Africa today. The swamp gradually turned into a coal bed, and the *Iguanodon* skeletons became fossils. Millions of years later, 24 of them were dug out of a coal mine in Belgium. A Belgian scientist, Louis Dollo, studied them and the surrounding fossils to learn more about *Iguanodon* and its environment.

 INSIDE STORY

Back to the Gobi

Scientists have known about the good dinosaur hunting grounds in the Gobi Desert, in Mongolia and China, since the first dinosaur expeditions in the 1920s. More dinosaur expeditions went to the Gobi during the 1980s. These were led by the paleontologists Philip Currie and Dale Russell from Canada, and Dong Zhiming from China.

Battling heat and ferocious desert sandstorms, the teams made some fantastic finds. They discovered the largest dinosaur that has ever been found in Asia, a sauropod called *Mamenchisaurus*. They dug up five different types of dinosaur eggs. And at one site, they found the skeletons of seven young armored dinosaurs called *Pinacosaurus*. These dinosaurs had huddled together in a sandstorm and been buried alive— 80 million years ago.

Head and neck bones

Tooth fossil

Word Builders

- *Paleo* means "ancient" or "from the distant past," while *ology* is "study of." So **paleontology** is "the study of the past."
- Botany is the study of plants. **Paleobotany** means "the study of ancient plants," using plant fossils.
- Another word for studying dinosaurs is paleozoology. Zoology is the study of animals, so **paleozoology** is "the study of ancient animals"—such as dinosaurs.

That's Amazing!

Dinosaur fossils were considered many things before they were finally recognized as dinosaur bones. In the 1600s, an English scientist thought that one particular dinosaur bone belonged to a giant human. In the early 1800s, some American scientists believed that trails of dinosaur footprints belonged to flocks of giant birds.

Pathfinder

- Where are the best places to find dinosaurs? Go to page 8.
- What did the first expeditions to the Gobi Desert find? Go to page 15.
- How have scientists changed their minds about what *Iguanodon* looked like? Go to pages 56–57.

HANDY *IGUANODON*

Scientists took a long time to figure out that *Iguanodon*'s large fossil spike belonged on its thumb, to be used like a dagger in defense. This was just one feature of *Iguanodon*'s amazing hands. Its three middle fingers had hooflike claws, to take its weight when walking. Its fifth finger could bend and grasp plants and other objects.

SOLVING A MYSTERY

GIDEON MANTELL

This English country doctor was an amateur paleontologist. He spent much of his life studying dinosaurs. His special discovery was *Iguanodon*, which he described in detail.

THE MYSTERY TEETH

Gideon's wife found some fossils in rocks in England. Gideon concluded they were teeth. In 1825, he decided they looked like the teeth of a modern iguana, except they were bigger. Gideon named his first dinosaur *Iguanodon*.

THE SLAB OF BONES

In 1834, some of Gideon's friends bought him the large slab of rock shown here. After studying the huge fossil bones it contained, Gideon realized that they were from the same animal as the fossil teeth he already had.

Tailbones

THE FIRST *IGUANODON*

Gideon studied the bones and teeth that he had and then drew this sketch. This is what he imagined *Iguanodon* would have looked like.

51

Hunting for a Dinosaur

WHEN YOU GO out hunting for a dinosaur, you must know where to look. Paleontologists usually start in places where fossils have already been found. The badlands of Wyoming, Montana, and South Dakota, U.S.A., have been searched again and again, because ongoing erosion can reveal new skeletons. At other times, paleontologists go to places where no one has looked before, but where the rocks are the right age and type to contain dinosaur fossils.

The paleontologists spend long hours walking through the area, their eyes fixed on the ground, looking for any sign that dinosaur bones are lurking below. Small bone chips are one sign. The chips can be scattered over a wide area. By following the trail of bone chips back to their origin, the paleontologists find the right spot to dig. Occasionally, they are really lucky and stumble on a whole skull or bones poking out of the ground, ready to collect.

Dinosaur fossils are very heavy but very fragile. Paleontologists spend long hours patiently digging with shovels, picks, brushes, and trowels to expose the fossils. Then the fossils are hardened with special chemicals and wrapped in plaster and burlap. Finally, they can be put onto waiting trucks for the journey to their new home.

DOWN IN THE BADLANDS
These badlands in North America are a hive of activity as a team of paleontologists excavates a Cretaceous bone bed. Some paleontologists carefully expose the remains of an almost complete hadrosaur in the foreground, while others map the skeleton before wrapping the individual bones in plaster and carrying them to a waiting truck. Another group is at work in the background, excavating a ceratopsian skeleton.

INSIDE STORY
The American Dinosaur Race

In the late 1800s, there was a dinosaur-bone race in the Wild West. Two of North America's greatest paleontologists, Othniel Charles Marsh (pictured in the middle of the back row) and Edward Drinker Cope, were in a rush to find the most dinosaur fossils.

They and their workers explored the Midwest in the U.S.A. for almost 30 years, digging up bigger and better fossils. They started out as friends but ended up as fierce rivals. They would even turn up at each other's excavations and pay off the workers to get hold of their rival's fossils. Between them, Marsh and Cope described and named 130 new dinosaur species, as well as many other fossil animals. Cope named more dinosaurs, but Marsh's discoveries were more accurate.

FROM SITE TO MUSEUM

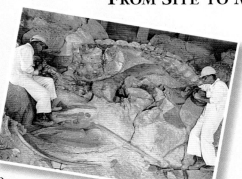

DIG IT
First, paleontologists chip away any dirt or rock covering the top of the fossil. Then they free it from the rock by cutting a deep trench in the rock all the way around the fossil. The rock can be so hard that paleontologists may have to use a drill to break it up.

MAP IT
Before any bones are moved, the paleontologists draw a detailed map of the site. This map shows exactly where each fossil bone and fragment was found, plus any other interesting details. This is an important guide for the paleontologists back at the laboratory.

Word Builders

Taphonomy is the study of what happens to an animal from the time it dies to the time it is dug up again as a fossil. The word comes from two Greek words—*taphe*, meaning "grave," and *nemo*, meaning "arrangement." A taphonomist studies the animal's fossilized bones and the surrounding rocks, which reveal a lot about the animal and its environment.

That's Amazing!

An animal often weighs more when it is dead and fossilized than it did when it was alive. That's because the minerals that replace the animal's bones and turn them into fossils are usually very heavy. Some fossilized skeletons can weigh many tons.

Pathfinder

• What huge dinosaur hunt had more than 500 people working at the site? Go to page 36.
• What did a hadrosaur look like? And a ceratopsian? Go to pages 34–37.
• How do dinosaur fossils form? Go to pages 46–47.

HANDS ON

Finding Fossils

Finding a fossil can be an adventure. First you need to find out where to look for fossils. Local and state museums will direct you to the nearest fossil sites. You will need a geologist's hammer, chisels, old newspaper in which to wrap your finds, and goggles to protect your eyes.

At the site, work carefully to break open rocks with your hammer and chisels. Fossils are usually found between flat planes of rock. Use trial and error to find the best way to open a particular rock to reveal any fossils. Chip away as much rock from around the fossil as you can without damaging it. Then take the fossil home, wrapped in newspaper.

You will likely find very common fossils, such as shellfish. But if you do find a bone or other rare fossil, notify your local museum and leave the rest of the excavation to the experts.

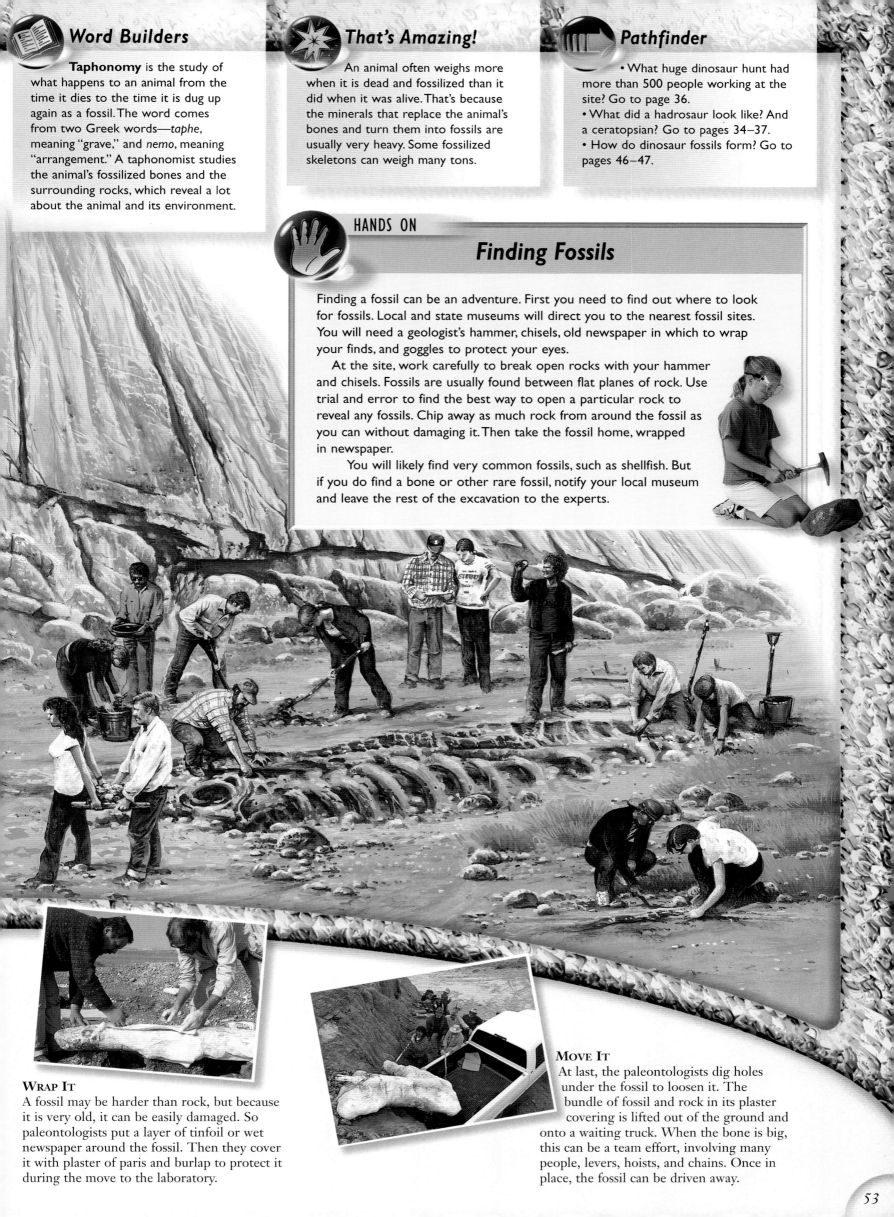

WRAP IT
A fossil may be harder than rock, but because it is very old, it can be easily damaged. So paleontologists put a layer of tinfoil or wet newspaper around the fossil. Then they cover it with plaster of paris and burlap to protect it during the move to the laboratory.

MOVE IT
At last, the paleontologists dig holes under the fossil to loosen it. The bundle of fossil and rock in its plaster covering is lifted out of the ground and onto a waiting truck. When the bone is big, this can be a team effort, involving many people, levers, hoists, and chains. Once in place, the fossil can be driven away.

Reconstructing a Dinosaur

THE FOSSILS ARE safely back in the laboratory. Now begin the hours of cleaning, conservation, and study to reconstruct the skeleton and identify the dinosaur.

Technicians get to work, cutting away the plaster and removing the newspaper or tinfoil layer from around the fossils. After brushing the fossils clean of dust and loose surface grit, technicians carefully remove any rock still attached to the fossil. The trick is to clean the fossil without doing any damage—with an array of fine chisels and saws, dental picks and drills, engraving tools, and small air-powered abrasive instruments. The technicians slowly free the skeleton from its rocky casing. Freshly exposed pieces of fossil are hardened and reinforced with glues or special plastics. Broken bones are glued together again. Finally, all the fossil bones are ready to be made into a skeleton.

The paleontologists now begin their detailed study of the specimen. As they put the bones together, they are on the lookout for any features that will help identify the dinosaur. They may even discover that they have a completely new type of dinosaur. If so, they give it a name and publish a full description of it. Everyone gets to hear about this new addition to the dinosaur group.

DINOSAUR ON DISPLAY

A technician puts the finishing touches to a carnosaur fossil, welding its metal supports together before it goes on display in a museum. Fossil bones are very heavy, so a strong metal frame is custom-built to support and connect each bone. Sometimes, steel wires are attached to the ceiling to hold up long necks or tails or big heads. Fossils are so heavy and so easily damaged that often the skeletons we see in museums are not the actual fossils. They are very clever fiberglass replicas.

Shoulder

Word Builders

Dinosaur technicians can specialize in different parts of the job of preparing fossils.
• Technicians that clean and restore fossils are called **preparators**.
• Those that harden fossils and prevent their decay are called **conservators**. Often, one technician can be both a preparator and a conservator. But big museums usually have both types of specialists in the different techniques.

That's Amazing!

Paleontologists learn a lot about extinct animals by looking at living ones. For example, the legs of an ostrich are not very different from a meat-eating dinosaur's. So by watching ostriches walk, paleontologists can get a good idea of how meat-eaters moved. Paleontologists also observe the breeding grounds and nesting behavior of living birds to imagine how dinosaurs cared for their young.

Pathfinder

• Why is it unusual to find a complete dinosaur skeleton? Go to pages 46–47.
• What did one of the earliest dinosaur reconstructions look like? Go to page 51.
• Where can you go to see dinosaur bone beds and watch technicians preparing fossils? Go to page 32.

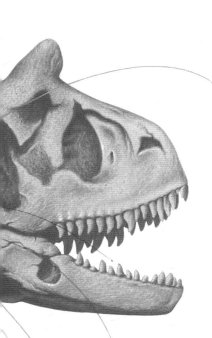

A Puzzle

Each fossil bone is a piece in the puzzle of a dinosaur. Long hours of patient study can solve the puzzle. Paleontologists often have only a few fragments of bone, so they must work out the shapes of all the missing bones and fit them together by looking at other dinosaur fossils.

 INSIDE STORY

Dinosaurs at the Smithsonian

You can visit one of the world's best collections of dinosaurs at the Smithsonian's National Museum of Natural History in Washington, D.C., U.S.A. As you walk through the series of galleries, you can explore the fossil exhibits of early plants and mammals. Then you enter the Hall of Dinosaurs.

The centerpiece of the hall is a huge skeleton of *Diplodocus*, more than 85 feet (26 m) long. Stalking beside it is a skeleton of meat-eating *Allosaurus*. The gallery is filled with other dinosaurs, including *Tyrannosaurus*, *Edmontosaurus*, and *Triceratops*. You can climb up to a balcony and look down on all the dinosaurs below. From here, you also get a good view of the skeletons mounted high on the opposite wall. Scenes recreate life in the Jurassic and Cretaceous periods, and show what the world would have looked like just before the dinosaurs disappeared.

Neck vertebra

CLEANING FOSSILS

Saw and Chisel Away
Technicians can spend months patiently freeing a fossil from its casing of rock, called the matrix. They start by removing as much of the rock as possible with hammers and fine chisels or pneumatic saws.

Blast Away
If the fossil bone is harder than sand, technicians can use a small shotblaster. Blasts of tiny sand particles erode the rock away. Or the technician may dip the fossil in an acid bath to free it from the rock.

Stuck Hard
The fossil needs to be hardened so it will be preserved forever. Technicians apply special glues and plastics to the fossil to make sure it won't fall apart.

Fine Finish
To remove the last bits of rock or to work on a fine fossil, technicians need a microscope. They may use an air-powered engraver, a scalpel, a dentist's drill—even a pin held in a hand vice—to finish the job.

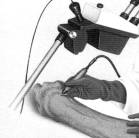

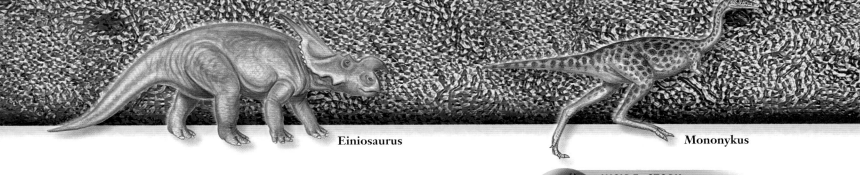

Einiosaurus

Mononykus

Brought Back to Life

TO RE-CREATE A dinosaur, paleontologists carefully study the complete fossil skeleton to make sure the bones are put together the right way. They look at the joint surfaces between the bones to work out how the dinosaur moved.

Now the paleontologists put some internal organs inside those bones—a brain, heart, stomach, lungs, and so on. But most dinosaur organs rotted before they could become fossils, so we don't really know what they were like. Paleontologists look at living dinosaur relatives such as crocodiles and birds for some clues. They do this again when they clothe the skeleton in muscles, adding many layers of muscles to give the dinosaur its body shape.

Then it's time for the finishing touch—the skin. Because there are some fossil impressions of dinosaur skin, paleontologists have a good idea of its texture. But they have to guess its color, because colors do not fossilize.

Paleontologists can know only some details about a dinosaur from its fossils. They can work out more details by comparing it with other dinosaur skeletons as well as certain animals alive today. They add a bit of guesswork and a good imagination. And that's how they bring a dinosaur that has been dead for millions of years back to life.

INSIDE STORY
Drawing Dinosaurs

Illustrations are an important part of re-creating a dinosaur. A dinosaur illustrator is a specialist who draws all the fossil bones of a new dinosaur skeleton. These drawings help tell the world about the new dinosaur.

The dinosaur illustrator also works with a paleontologist to create an image of what the newly discovered dinosaur looked like. They discuss the fossils and everything that is known about the dinosaur and its environment. The illustrator then makes sketches of the dinosaur. After more discussions with the paleontologist, the illustrator uses color to bring the dinosaur to life.

THE BONES
The complete skeleton is constructed. Broken bones are glued together. Fiberglass replacements are made for missing bones. *Giganotosaurus* was missing some tail bones, but the paleontologists could model new ones by looking at a close relative such as *Allosaurus*.

A MODEL DINOSAUR
Thanks to modern robotics, we can build realistic, life-sized models of dinosaurs that move just like the real thing. These dino-robots even roar and grunt. We don't know what sounds dinosaurs really made, but we can always guess.

CHANGING *IGUANODON*
LIKE AN IGUANA
A dinosaur's appearance changes as new studies and theories appear. When this sculpture was made in 1853, scientists thought *Iguanodon* was like a giant iguana, with a spike on its nose.

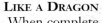

LIKE A DRAGON
When complete skeletons of *Iguanodon* were dug up in the late 1800s, scientists learned it could walk on two legs and that the spike was a daggerlike thumb claw. But they imagined that such a big animal would be like a dragon.

Word Builders

The scientific name for an animal can be used only once. Occasionally, a name is given to two different animals, so one has to have a name change. **Mononychus** means "one claw." It was the name given to a small theropod that had a single claw on each small arm. But a beetle already had that name, so the theropod got a new name, **Mononykus,** which also means "one claw."

That's Amazing!

Sometimes the bones of two different dinosaurs get mixed up. This happened to "Brontosaurus," which had the skeleton of an *Apatosaurus* with the head from another dinosaur. Nobody realized the mistake for decades, and "Brontosaurus" became famous. But in the early 1990s, the correct head was put on the specimen in the American Museum of Natural History, and "Brontosaurus" was no more.

Pathfinder

• When was *Giganotosaurus* the king of the dinosaurs? Go to page 40.
• How did the man who discovered *Iguanodon* imagine it looked, when he only had some teeth and a few bones? Go to page 51.
• Are birds close relatives of the dinosaurs? Go to pages 60–61.

THE SKIN

No *Giganotosaurus* skin has ever been found, but rare fossils of other dinosaurs' skin do exist. Paleontologists create its skin by looking at these fossils and at living reptiles such as crocodiles and lizards. To get the color, they guess, based on animals that live in similar environments today.

THE ORGANS

Dinosaurs' internal organs turn into fossils only in the most exceptional circumstances. Usually, they are too soft to be preserved. So scientists mostly have to guess about the position and size of *Giganotosaurus*'s heart, lungs, intestines, and other organs. Their guesses are helped by studying living relatives such as crocodiles and birds.

THE MUSCLES

Millions of years ago, the muscles of *Giganotosaurus* left scars where they connected to its bones. By reading the scars on the bones, scientists can work out how big the muscles were and how they were positioned. To get *Giganotosaurus*'s body shape, scientists add layers of muscles.

Giganotosaurus

CREATIVE COLOR

We don't know what colors dinosaurs were. But illustrators can try out ideas. Maybe the frill of a horned dinosaur had circles like a bull's eye, to look bigger and more scary. Or maybe it was really colorful to attract mates. Perhaps it was drab, for good camouflage.

LIKE A REPTILE

In later re-creations of *Iguanodon*, it started looking less like a dragon and more like a gigantic reptile. But it was seen as sluggish and so big and heavy that it needed to rest on its tail.

LIKE AN *IGUANODON*

The modern reconstruction of this dinosaur is very different from when it was first found. We now think that *Iguanodon* was very active. It usually walked on all fours, carrying its tail up in the air.

When the Dinosaurs Died

AFTER RULING EARTH for 160 million years, the dinosaurs suddenly vanished 65 million years ago. This was one of the most mysterious disappearances in the Earth's history. But dinosaurs were not the only ones to die out at the end of the Cretaceous period. Thousands of other animals became extinct. In the oceans, some fish survived, but all the marine reptiles died except the turtles. In the air, the pterosaurs didn't make it, while the birds and insects did. On land, the dinosaurs vanished, but the other reptile groups—the crocodiles, lizards, snakes, and tortoises—continued, along with the amphibians and the mammals. Almost half the plants that thrived during the Cretaceous period were no longer growing in the Tertiary period.

The catastrophic event that caused this mass extinction had to be powerful enough to decimate 75 percent of all the animals and plants but still leave some things alive. It was so long ago that it's hard to prove what happened. Scientists have a number of theories. Some believe there were major changes in the weather or a volcanic disaster. The main theory is that a huge meteorite collided with Earth, causing environmental chaos around the world. The dinosaurs, along with many other animals and plants, were wiped out.

A SURVIVOR
Mammals such as this *Purgatorius* were some of the animals that survived the mass extinction. Cretaceous mammals were small, so maybe they burrowed and hid away from the worst effects. They soon evolved into thousands of new species and replaced the dinosaurs as the ruling animals of Earth. Birds, insects, fish, crocodiles, amphibians, turtles, tortoises, snakes, and lizards also survived.

INSIDE STORY

If a Meteorite Hit

A rock bigger than Mount Everest and spinning through outer space at 30,000 miles (50,000 km) per hour slammed into Earth at the end of the Cretaceous period. It left a massive crater, like the one pictured below, but much bigger. The Earth's atmosphere ignited, half the world was ablaze, and the air filled with thick smoke and dust. Acid rain started pouring down, dissolving everything that it touched. The sun was completely blocked out, so plants stopped growing. Many animals that survived the blast, the fires, and the acid rain soon died from starvation because there was nothing for them to eat.

This is what many paleontologists think is the best explanation for what caused the mass extinction that brought the Cretaceous period and the Age of Dinosaurs to an end.

METEORITE STRIKE
The sky is set alight when a massive meteorite crashes into Earth. Fire burns everything for thousands of miles, including this *Triceratops*. *Triceratops* was one of the types of dinosaurs that lived right up until the end of the Cretaceous period. *Tyrannosaurus*, *Edmontosaurus*, and *Pachycephalosaurus* also survived until the mass extinction.

• What were the marine reptiles and pterosaurs? Go to pages 24–25.
• How did dinosaurs control their body temperature? Go to pages 18–19.
• What was the world like in the Cretaceous period, before the mass extinction? Go to pages 14–15.

MORE EXTINCTION THEORIES

FUNNY THEORIES

One of the silliest theories for why dinosaurs disappeared is that aliens from outer space kidnapped them. Other theories claim the dinosaurs died of boredom, or they drowned in their dung, or they were just too dumb to survive. We know this wasn't so.

HOT CLIMATE CHANGE

Maybe the world's climate heated up. Food became more scarce in the harsh conditions. Larger animals such as dinosaurs had trouble keeping cool, and they died of excess heat.

COOL CLIMATE CHANGE

Maybe the climate got too cold. Dinosaurs couldn't keep warm or get enough to eat because many plants could not grow. Freezing and starving, the dinosaurs eventually died out.

Turtle

VOLCANIC ERUPTIONS

Maybe a series of massive volcanic eruptions poisoned the atmosphere and clouded the skies. With no sunlight getting through the clouds, plants couldn't grow. Plant-eaters starved, leaving meat-eaters to starve and die out, too.

Dinosaur Relatives Today

DINOSAURS ARE DEAD, but some of their relatives—birds and crocodiles—are alive today. Scientists believe the first bird was *Archaeopteryx*, and it appeared during the Jurassic period. It was an evolutionary offshoot from a group of small, meat-eating dinosaurs. Some of these dinosaurs, such as *Caudipteryx* and *Sinosauropteryx*, even had feathers, but not for flying. The fossils of these feathered meat-eaters clearly show the link between dinosaurs and birds.

Birds today don't look much like their dinosaur ancestors, but they still share certain features. The most obvious is their feet. Birds have three toes pointing forward and a fourth toe pointing backward. The feet of meat-eating dinosaurs were the same. Look at a chicken and you will see that its feet are similar in shape to those of *Tyrannosaurus*. Some scientists even say that dinosaurs are still alive because birds are really dinosaurs and they are still living.

The other dinosaur relatives alive today, the crocodiles, have very similar skulls to dinosaurs. Both share early archosaur ancestors. Unlike the dinosaurs, however, crocodiles did not die out 65 million years ago. They have hardly changed since then, and can teach us many things about their extinct relatives.

DISTANT COUSINS

With its long, wavy smile and big, snaggly teeth, the meat-eating dinosaur *Baryonyx* had a head very similar to a crocodile's. *Baryonyx* and crocodiles were very distant cousins. Their jaws look alike because they probably did the same job—catch fish.

INSIDE STORY

The First Bird

In 1861, miners working in a limestone quarry near Solnhofen in southern Germany uncovered a beautifully preserved fossil feather. This discovery caused a sensation. Scientists had previously thought that birds were not so very old, but the fossil feather was 145 million years old. The paleontologist Hermann von Meyer named the unknown owner of this single feather *Archaeopteryx*. Then the miners found an almost complete fossil of an *Archaeopteryx*. Its skeleton looked like that of a small, meat-eating dinosaur. But its body was covered in finely detailed feathers, and it had birdlike wings.

With this mix of features, *Archaeopteryx* shows the direct link between the dinosaurs and the birds. And at 145 million years old, it is also the earliest known bird.

FOSSIL WITH FEATHERS

Caudipteryx was a feathered dinosaur. Its fossil, including the faint marks of its feathers, was recently discovered in China. The long feathers on its hands and tail were not for flying. They were probably used for display, or perhaps to trap and catch insects.

Word Builders

Pteryx is Greek for "wing" or "feather." The word can be found in some dinosaur and bird names.
• *Archaeo* means "ancient," so **Archaeopteryx** means "ancient wing."
• *Caudal* means "tail," so **Caudipteryx** means "tail feather."
• *Sino* means "Chinese." **Sinosauropteryx** means "Chinese lizard with feathers." This dinosaur with feathers was found in China.

That's Amazing!

The first person to recognize the relationship between dinosaurs and birds was the British paleontologist Thomas Huxley. As Huxley ate partridge one night, he thought about a dinosaur ankle bone that had been puzzling him for some time. Looking at the ankle of the bird he was eating, he realized that it was exactly the same bone. This led him to theorize that dinosaurs and birds were relatives.

Pathfinder

• Why did birds evolve from the dinosaurs with lizardlike hips and not from the dinosaurs with birdlike hips? Go to page 17.
• What creatures flew before birds? Go to pages 24–25.
• What dinosaurs looked like ostriches and could run almost as fast? Go to pages 42–43.

FAMILY TREE
Alligators and crocodiles are archosaurs, just as dinosaurs were. The dinosaurs evolved into two main groups—ornithischians and saurischians. Birds evolved from saurischian dinosaurs. Alligators, crocodiles, and birds survive today.

Archosaurs
Alligators and crocodiles
Ornithischian dinosaurs
Saurischian dinosaurs
Birds
Triassic Jurassic Cretaceous Tertiary Quaternary

RUN, FLAP, LEAP, FLY
Archaeopteryx runs along the ground, flapping its feathered wings to get a little extra lift as it chases an insect. *Archaeopteryx* is thought to have been the first bird. Dinosaurs probably had feathers to help keep them warm. Later, when *Archaeopteryx* evolved from the dinosaurs, its feathers grew longer so it could fly after prey.

Secretary bird

FROM DINOSAUR TO BIRD

Small meat-eating dinosaurs such as *Compsognathus* ran around on their two back legs, leaving their arms free to catch prey. The first bird, *Archaeopteryx*, turned this grasping movement into a flapping movement by using its early wings. Modern birds have lost the claws on the wings, the long bony tail, and the teeth of this ancient bird. Flapping has become soaring flight.

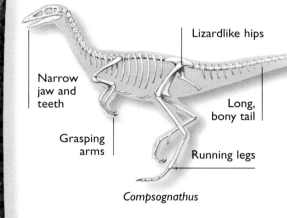

Narrow jaw and teeth
Grasping arms
Lizardlike hips
Long, bony tail
Running legs

Compsognathus

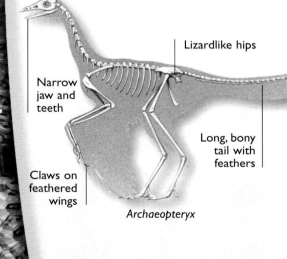

Narrow jaw and teeth
Claws on feathered wings
Lizardlike hips
Long, bony tail with feathers

Archaeopteryx

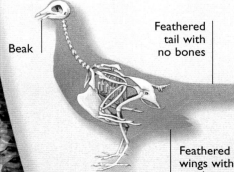

Beak
Feathered tail with no bones
Feathered wings with no claws

Modern Bird

Plant fossil   Ichthyosaurus, *an ichthyosaur*   *Iguanodont trackway*

Glossary

ankylosaurs A group of armored plant-eating dinosaurs that lived in North America, Asia, Europe, and Australia by the late Cretaceous period. Their barrel-shaped bodies were protected by thick plates of bone and rows of spikes.

archosaurs A major group of reptiles. It includes the crocodiles and alligators, archosaurs that are still alive. It also includes the extinct dinosaurs and pterosaurs.

badlands The landscape where many dinosaur fossils are found. Badlands are often remote and barren areas where rivers and wind have eroded layers of rock to reveal fossils. There are badlands in Montana, Utah, Wyoming, Colorado, and New Mexico in the United States; in Alberta in Canada; in Patagonia in South America; and in the Gobi Desert in China and Mongolia.

bipedal Traveling on two legs.

bone bed A layer of rock full of fossil bones. You can see a bone bed at Dinosaur Provincial Park in Canada. Thousands of ceratopsians drowned there crossing a river in the Cretaceous period. Their bodies turned into a bed of fossilized bones.

camouflage A way of disguising something so that it blends with or remains hidden in its environment. Some dinosaurs' skin may have been the same color as their environment, to camouflage them from their prey or other predators.

carnivore An animal or a plant that eats meat.

carnosaurs A group of massive, powerful, meat-eating theropods, like *Allosaurus* and *Giganotosaurus*. Some could grow bigger than a dump truck. They were active hunters that probably scavenged when they could. Because of their size and weight, they couldn't run very fast or far.

ceratopsians A group of four-legged plant-eaters such as *Triceratops*. Their large heads had horns and bony neck frills. They were one of the last groups of dinosaurs to evolve, spreading in huge herds throughout North America and Asia, browsing and traveling over the plains.

coelurosaurs The most famous of the meat-eating dinosaurs. They ranged in size from 10-foot (3-m) *Coelophysis* to 40-foot (12-m) *Tyrannosaurus*. They were most common in the Cretaceous period, and birds evolved from them.

cold-blooded Animals such as snakes and lizards are called "cold-blooded." They get their body heat from the outside environment, by sitting in the sun. On a cold day they are less active.

coprolite A dinosaur dropping that has become a fossil.

Cretaceous period The third and last geological period of the Mesozoic era. It lasted from 144 to 65 million years ago, when a great variety of dinosaurs evolved and then became extinct.

erosion The wearing away of the Earth's surface by rivers, rain, waves, glaciers, or winds.

evolution The changing of plants and animals over millions of years. Dinosaurs evolved from their ancestors and then evolved into different species during the 183 million years of the Mesozoic era.

excavation Uncovering something and then digging it out of the ground. Any kind of fossil has to be excavated very carefully.

extinction The dying-out of a species. Dinosaurs became extinct at the end of the Cretaceous period. Their close relatives, the birds, did not.

fossil Any evidence of pre-existing life. It may be the remains of a plant or animal that have turned to stone or have left their impression on rock.

gastroliths Stomach stones. The sauropods swallowed these stones to help digest food in their stomachs.

hadrosaurs A group of duck-billed, plant-eating dinosaurs such as *Parasaurolophus* and *Edmontosaurus*. They had broad, ducklike beaks and batteries of grinding teeth. Many had bony head crests with unusual shapes. They first evolved in Asia during the early Cretaceous period, and became the most common and the most varied ornithopods of that period.

herbivore An animal that eats only plants.

ichthyosaurs One of the groups of marine reptiles living at the same time as the dinosaurs. They had dolphin-shaped bodies, and gave birth to live young in the sea.

iguanodonts Large, plant-eating dinosaurs such as *Iguanodon* that mostly walked on four feet. They first appeared during the Jurassic period and became widespread during the early Cretaceous period.

Jurassic period The middle geological period of the Mesozoic era. It lasted from 208 to 144 million years ago. The conditions on Earth were just right for new types of dinosaurs to flourish, particularly the huge, long-necked sauropods.

mammals A group of backboned animals that have hair or fur and feed their young on milk. Humans are mammals. So are dogs, cats, and bats.

matrix The rock still attached to a fossil after it has been dug out of the ground. The matrix is carefully removed from around the fossil by skilled technicians in the laboratory.

Edmontosaurus, *a hadrosaur*   Dryosaurus, *a small ornithopod*

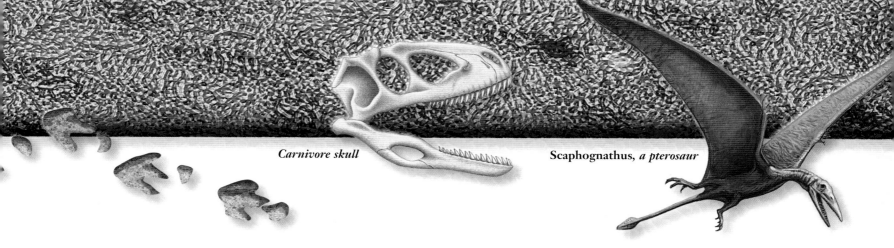

Carnivore skull

Scaphognathus, a pterosaur

Mesozoic era The Age of Dinosaurs. It began 245 million years ago, before dinosaurs had evolved, and ended 65 million years ago with a mass extinction of plants and animals. It spanned the Triassic, Jurassic, and Cretaceous periods.

meteorite A mass of rock or metal that has fallen to Earth. It comes from an asteroid in outer space.

migration A number of animals moving from one region to another, perhaps to breed or to find food during winter or summer. Hadrosaurs and ceratopsians migrated across North America in vast herds.

mosasaurs Marine lizards also known as sea dragons. They lived in inshore waters during the late Cretaceous period. They had thick, eel-shaped bodies with four flippers.

mummified Dried out by heat or wind. Some dinosaurs were preserved in this way, after being buried in a sandstorm or volcanic ash. Even their skin and organs may have been fossilized.

ornithischians The bird-hipped dinosaurs. They had a hip structure where the pubis bone pointed backward, parallel to the ischium. All ornithischians were plant-eaters.

ornithopods The bird-footed, bird-hipped dinosaurs. These plant-eaters included some of the oldest and most successful dinosaur families, like the iguanodonts and hadrosaurs.

pachycephalosaurs The boneheads, a group of plant-eating dinosaurs with skulls thickened into domes of bone. They included *Pachycephalosaurus* and *Prenocephale*. Most lived during the late Cretaceous period in North America and Asia.

paleontologist A scientist who learns about ancient life forms by studying fossils of plants and animals.

plesiosaurs Large marine reptiles that flourished during the Jurassic and Cretaceous periods. Their long necks could rise above the sea's surface. They swam through the water using their four paddlelike flippers.

pliosaurs Marine reptiles that had large heads with strong teeth, short necks, and sturdy, streamlined bodies. They were the killers of the Mesozoic seas.

predator An animal that hunts or preys on other animals for its food.

prosauropods One of the earliest groups of dinosaurs. These saurischian plant-eaters, such as *Plateosaurus*, lived during the late Triassic and early Jurassic periods.

pterosaurs Flying reptiles such as *Scaphognathus* that first appeared during the late Triassic period.

quadrupedal Traveling on four legs.

reptiles A group of backboned animals. They have scaly skin, and their young hatch out of eggs. Snakes and lizards are modern-day reptiles.

saurischians The lizard-hipped dinosaurs. They had a hip structure where the pubis bone pointed forward. All meat-eaters were saurischians. The plant-eating prosauropods and sauropods were also saurischians.

sauropods The quadrupedal dinosaurs such as *Diplodocus* and *Brachiosaurus* with very long necks and tails. They were one of the two types of plant-eaters with lizardlike hips— most plant-eaters had birdlike hips. Evolving in the late Triassic period, they included the largest animals ever to walk Earth.

scavenger A meat-eating animal that feeds on dead animals. It either waits until the hunter has eaten its fill, or it steals the dead animal from the hunter.

species A group of animals or plants that have common features. A group of similar species forms a genus. *Tyrannosaurus rex* was a species of the *Tyrannosaurus* genus of dinosaurs.

stegosaurs Four-legged, plant-eating dinosaurs with bony plates along their backs, and pairs of long, sharp spikes on the end of their strong tails. From the late Jurassic period, they roamed North America, Europe, Asia, and Africa, and included *Stegosaurus* and *Kentrosaurus*.

synapsids A group of animals that appeared with reptiles. They lived before the dinosaurs, and mammals evolved from them.

therizinosaurs A group of exotic dinosaurs that were theropods but had some features similar to prosauropods. They included *Segnosaurus* and *Erlikosaurus*, and lived during the Cretaceous period.

theropods All the meat-eating dinosaurs. They were lizard-hipped and walked on their back legs.

trackways A series of footprints left by an animal walking or running over soft ground. Some dinosaur trackways became fossilized.

Triassic period The first geological period in the Mesozoic era, from 248 to 208 million years ago. Dinosaurs first appeared about halfway through this period, around 228 million years ago.

vertebrae The bones along the spine, from the base of the skull to the tail. They protect the spinal column.

warm-blooded Animals such as mammals and birds are called "warm-blooded." Their body temperature stays about the same, because they generate heat inside their bodies from the food they eat. They can be active all the time.

Sauropod skeleton

Scutellosaurus, an ornithischian

Index

The publishers would like to thank the following people for their assistance in the preparation of this book: Barbara Bakowski, James Clark, Dina Rubin, and Jennifer Themel.
Our special thanks to the following children who feature in the photographs: Michelle Burk, Elliot Burton, Lisa Chan, Anton Crowden and Henry (dog), Gemma Smith, Gerard Smith, Andrew Tout, Lucy Vaux.
PICTURE CREDITS (t=top, b=bottom, l=left, r=right, c=center, e=extreme, f=flap, F=Front, C=Cover, B=Back) (NHM=Natural History Museum, TPL=The Photo Library, Sydney, SPL=Science Photo Library, UOC=University of Chicago.)
Ad-Libitum 5b, 9br, 14l, 16l, 19tr, 22r, 27l, 28l, 33tr, 33b, 37cr, 39b, 44b, 52t, 53tr (M. Kaniewski). **American Museum of Natural History** 15c. **Ardea London Ltd**, 13c (P. Morris), 31tl, 8l (F. Gohier). **Auscape** 56l (D. Parer & E. Parer-Cook), 10l, 37tr, 38tl, 38tr, 40r, 46c, 53br, 60l (F. Gohier), 48l (S. Wilby & C. Ciantar). **Australian Museum** 47tl (Nature Focus). **Brigham Young University** 39c (M.A. Philbrick). **Dinosaur National Monument, Utah**, 52bc. **Everett Collection** 12c, 24l. **James Farlow** 43r. **David Gillette** 30bl. **The Granger Collection** 51tr. **Jeff Foott Prod.BC** 32bl. **Museum of the Rockies** 22bl (B. Selyem). **National Geographic Society** 55b (J. Amos). **NHM** 25tl, 28c, 28r, 31tr, 32tr, 34c, 42bl, 43br, 48r, 48t, 51c, 51r, 51bl, 53bl, 55t, 56bl. **Palaontologisches Museum Universtat Zu Berlin** 36bl. **Peabody Museum of Natural History** 18bl, 52cl. **TPL** 8tl (A. Evrard), 50t (Hulton-Deutsch), 9r (SPL/P. Plailly), 34t (K. Schaffer). **Dr. Robert Reid, UK** 18br, 19bl, 19br. **UOC** 11c (P. Sereno) US Geological Survey, 58l. **Wave Productions** 45tr, 56r (O. Strewe). **Paul Willis** 21tr.
ILLUSTRATION CREDITS
Anne Bowman 44t, 46tl, 46tr, 60tl. **Jimmy Chan** 40l, 59tl. **Simone End** 6ebr, 9tc, 13tr, 13c, 13r, 16tr, 24br, 35c, 35r, 42tl, 42tc. **John Francis/Bernard Thornton Artists UK** 20br. **Murray Frederick** 44r, 48/49c, 48t, 48bl, 48br, 49tl, 49r, 49bl, 62tr. **Lee Gibbons/Wildlife Art Ltd** 45c,

58/59c, 58r, 59r. **Ray Grinaway** 13c, 13br, 47tr. **Jim Harter (ed.) Animals** (Dover, 1979) 56br, 57bl. **Gino Hasler** 5r, 26cr, 27r, 30bl, 30br, 31bl, 31bc, 31br, 40tl, 40tc, 40tr, 40bl, 40br, 41tr, 41cr, 41br, 63tc. **Tim Hayward/Bernard Thornton Artists UK** 58bl. **David Kirshner** 7tl, 7c, 16/17c, 16etr, 16tl, 16r, 16b, 17t, 17r, 17bl, 17br, 18/19c, 18tr, 19br, 26r, 27l, 32/33c, 32tl, 32tc, 32tr, 32b, 33r, 33br, 38/39c, 38r, 45l, 45br, 56/57c, 56tl, 56tr, 57r, 57br, 58tr, 58br, 59bl, 60er, 63bl. **Frank Knight** 4tr, 6tr, 9tl, 10bl, 10br, 11bc, 11br, 20r, 24tl, 25bc, 25bl, 40c, 46/47b. **David McAllister** 52/53c, 52br. **James McKinnon** 4cr, 6r, 6br, 10/11c, 10tl, 10tr, 11cr, 11tr, 11bl, 12/13c, 12tl, 12tc, 12tr, 27tl, 27tr, 36tl, 36tc, 36tr, 36bl, 36br, 37c, 37bl, 37bc, 37br, 37eb, 44c, 50tl, 50tr, 50l, 50bl, 50br, 51tl, 51c, 51b, 63tr, 63br. **Stuart McVicar** (digital manipulation) 6cr, 10r, 12r, 14r. **Colin Newman/Bernard Thornton Artists UK** 9tr, 23t, 58br. **Luis Rey/Wildlife Art Ltd** 7cl, 14/15c, 14tl, 14bl, 14br, 15cr, 15br, 20/21c, 20tl, 20tc, 20tr, 20b, 21r, 21bl, 21br, 27c, 28/29c, 28tl, 28tr, 28bl, 28br, 29r, 29bc, 41c, 62bl, 62br. **Peter Schouten** 4r, 8c, 8/9c, 8/9b, 12bl, 12br, 14tr, 15b, 18tl, 26tr, 27br, 29tr, 29br, 30/31c, 30tl, 30tc, 30tr, 30tc, 42tr, 42c, 62tl. **Peter Scott/Wildlife Art Ltd** 7br, 22tl, 22tc, 22tr, 22br, 23c, 23bl, 23br, 26br, 27bl, 34/35c, 34tl, 34tc, 34tr, 34bl, 35l, 35cr, 35bl, 35bc, 35br, 42/43c, 42tr, 42l, 42bl, 42br, 43bl, 45bl, 60tr, 60c, 60r, 60bl, 60br, 61t, 61r, 61bl **Marco Sparaciari** 4br, 45tl, 54tl, 54tc, 54tr, 54c, 54bl, 55r, 55bl, 55br. **Kevin Stead** 7l, 7bl, 13cr, 24/25c, 24tc, 24tr, 24c, 24bl, 25tr, 25r, 25bl, 46/47c, 58tl, 62tc. **Ann Winterbotham** 15tr.
COVER CREDITS
Ad-Libitum Fcbr, Ffcb, BCcr (M. Kaniewski). **Gino Hasler** FCbc, **David Kirshner** Bftr, **James McKinnon** Fctr, Ffct, BCtc, BCbl, **Luis Rey/Wildlife Art Ltd** FCc, BCtr, BCr, BCbr, BCb, BCl, BCcl, **Peter Schouten** FCbr, Bfb, **Peter Scott/Wildlife Art Ltd** FCtl, FCl, FCr, FCbl, Fft, Ffb, BCtl, Bftl, Bfcr, Bfcl, **Kevin Stead** FCcr, BCc.

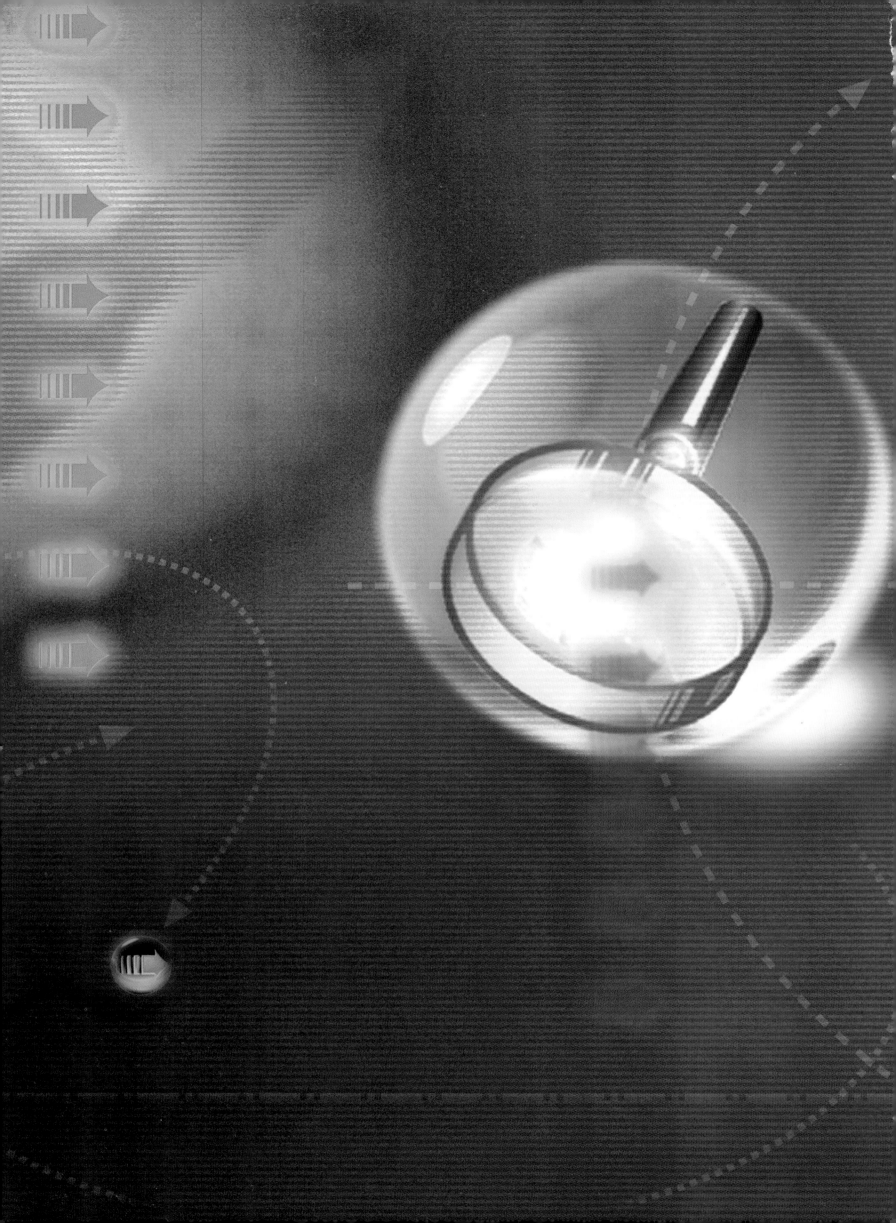